How to B Effective Compliance Officer

LEARN THE SECRETS OF INFLUENCE,
MOTIVATION AND PERSUASION TO BECOME AN
IN-DEMAND BUSINESS ASSET

Kristy Grant-Hart

Brentham House Publishing Company Ltd.
Covent Garden

HOW TO BE A WILDLY EFFECTIVE COMPLIANCE OFFICER

Brentham House Publishing Company
71-75 Shelton Street
Covent Garden
London, WC2H 9JQ

Brentham House Publishing Company books may be purchased for educational, business or sales promotional use. For information, please email the Special Markets Department at Info@BrenthamHousePublishing.com.

FIRST EDITION
A CIP Record of this book is available from the British Library.

ISBN: 978-0-9934788-0-2 (soft cover edition)
ISBN: 978-0-9934788-1-9 (electronic edition)

Praise for How to Be a Wildly Effective Compliance Officer:

"Kristy Grant-Hart infectiously describes the missing link in the compliance profession — interpersonal skills and influence. If you are or want to be a successful compliance professional — this book is invaluable."

Roy Snell
CEO Society of Corporate Compliance and Ethics

"Kristy Grant-Hart brings a fresh and inspiring perspective to compliance officers everywhere. Her candor and innovative approach can be easily adopted to improve compliance programs throughout the world. Run, don't walk, to get yourself a copy and become wildly effective!"

Lisa Beth Lentini, JD/MBA/LLM, CCEP certified
Vice President, Global Compliance, Carlson Wagonlit Travel

"Kristy Grant-Hart provides the most positive and motivating strategies to ensure successful buy-in from the business for any Compliance or Operational Risk professional to become Wildly Effective!"

Lisa Hall
Operational Risk Manager, Stifel

Contents

For my father, Kerry S. Grant, who always believed in my dreams and is here with me every step of the way.

Foreword

The men and women working in the compliance and ethics profession are heroes. You may not think of yourself this way; after all, most of your working day is probably filled with meetings, email and policy writing. But whether you are an internal investigator, trainer, outside consultant, internal auditor, inside counsel or any of the hundreds of jobs affiliated with the compliance and ethics profession, you are doing work that is changing the world.

Consider what we do for society and the potential victims of corporate misconduct. One reason for the prevalence of this type of misconduct is that those of us in companies are typically far removed from the victims of corporate wrongdoing. But those victims are very real.

If you think about it, this is also what we do. We make it so a little girl sees her father that night, instead of learning that he was killed on the job.

We make it so that people living in a small village are not suddenly killed by noxious gases released through plant negligence.

We make it so a family of four does not have their lives ruined by a horrendous car accident from defective parts.

We make it so a terrorist does not kill a group of young people with a bomb plot that was funded through money laundering.

We make it so a bridge does not collapse as a result of corrupt contracting.

We make it so a young, rising star manager does not ruin her career through a discussion with a competitor that would land her in jail.

"How to Be a Wildly Effective Compliance Officer" is filled with strategies and tips that will help you to be more successful, persuasive and influential in your job. It focuses on the person-to-person aspect of the profession and provides you with the ability to reach your audience in a profound and emotional way. Remember why this matters. By being the most effective professional that you can be, you will make a difference in the lives of real people.

- Joe Murphy

Author, "501 Ideas for Your Compliance & Ethics Program" and Editor-in-Chief of Compliance & Ethics Professional Magazine.

Introduction: How to Be a Wildly Effective Compliance Officer

"In response to being caught for our gigantic fraud, bribery, sanctions, and ethics failure, our company has agreed with the regulator to hire 4,000 more people into our Compliance Department. This is, of course, in addition to the 2,000 people we had working there during the time the scandalous behavior took place, and in addition to the 3,000 other people we hired into the Compliance Department after we entered into the Deferred Prosecution Agreement." -- CEO.

We see this every day in the news. Compliance departments continue to grow, but why aren't they more successful? Why doesn't hiring twice as many people mean twice as much monitoring and twice as much compliant behavior by the business? Is it simply a lack of resources that keeps compliance officers less effective than they could be? Or is it something else? Is the lack of training in human psychology, sales techniques, persuasion and motivation the reason? Could lack of information be the real thing stopping otherwise bright and dedicated employees from quintupling their effectiveness, moving from box-ticking compliance officers to

Wildly Effective ones with the right information? The answer is yes, and this book will help you do just that.

The Compliance profession has exploded in the last few years. U.S. News and World Report lists "compliance officer" as the No. 20 best business job in the country and notes that the Bureau of Labor Statics projects the occupation will grow by 4.6% through 2022[1].

In 2014, the Financial Times declared that "the age of the compliance officer arrive[d]." The newspaper noted that 70,000 new full-time jobs would be created in Europe alone to comply with the Basel III regulations for banks and that "tens of thousands of full-time positions" would be created in the United States in response to the new Dodd-Frank rules.[2] The Society of Corporate Compliance and Ethics and its sister organization, the Health Care Compliance Association, now boast tens of thousands of members.[3]

In response to each scandal, companies are hiring compliance officers and other compliance professionals. In 2013, JP Morgan Chase reported that more than 4,000 people had been assigned to risk, compliance, legal and finance, and that 3,000 of those compliance professionals had been hired that year. An extra $1 billion was being spent on controls, and the staff had undergone 750,000 hours of training on compliance issues.[4] That same year, HSBC hired 3,000 more compliance officers, making their compliance department 5,000 strong throughout the world.[5]

Compliance is growing as a profession globally as regulators work together to target multi-national companies in prosecutions. Risk is not limited to the United States and Europe, but is increasingly a global issue, requiring local professionals with language skills and knowledge of local laws. As a result, the compliance departments of banks, pharmaceutical companies, entertainment companies, and companies in all other industries are seeing the creation of a mini-army of compliance officers.

But what about you? This book isn't about the compliance profession as a whole. Instead, this book is meant to make YOU a Wildly Effective compliance officer. This book isn't about the law, or how to build a great compliance program that complies with the seven elements noted in the United States Federal Sentencing Guidelines. There are fantastic books that can help you with those things, but this book isn't one of them. Instead, this book is about YOU becoming as effective as you can be at your job.

Why did you become a compliance officer in the first place? Although some people fall into the role accidentally, most people join the compliance and ethics profession at least partially because they are deeply committed to making the world a better place. Many people in the compliance profession have a profound innate commitment to doing the right thing. Unfortunately, this commitment can often be seen by the outside world as something to be snickered at or ignored.

What's worse, many compliance officers haven't been trained on how to do their job effectively. Compliance officers tend to come from the ranks of auditors, finance professionals, lawyers, and other professions where logic and evidence are more important than influence. Many businesses view compliance as a necessary evil — something that must be tolerated instead of embraced. Leaders pay lip service to the importance of compliance, but do little to create incentives to encourage an ethical culture. In the worst cases, compliance is side-lined, creating a "check-the-box" culture where compliance obligations are hurdles to be overcome as quickly as possible.

Are You in the Compliance Compartment or Department?

Most modern companies have a compliance function. Some companies have a Compliance "compartment" where compliance is kept inside a small box, instead of a Compliance Department that sits with the business in a place of importance. In some companies, Compliance is treated as a compartmentalized separate entity that is not part of the core activity of the company. People working in Compliance Compartments often feel marginalized and angry at the lack of respect they receive from managers and colleagues. If you work in a Compliance Compartment, take heart.

This book is meant to teach you how to move from the Compliance Compartment into the Compliance Department, where the business will include you as a crucial part of the operation.

How this Book Will Help YOU

I wrote this book to help compliance officers go from being good at the technical aspects of their job to being Wildly Effective at their position. Many people in the compliance profession see their job as a function. Instead of being a function, I will teach you to be a business partner with influence and a capacity to get things done by leveraging the power sources in your company.

> *Instead of being a function, I will teach you to be a business partner with influence and a capacity to get things done by leveraging the power sources in your company.*

Each chapter of How to Be a Wildly Effective Compliance Officer gives you specific and actionable techniques that can be immediately implemented to increase efficacy. This book begins with the exploration of a critical requirement: you need a belief in the program that you are selling (yes, selling). I'll show you the framework that will be the foundation of everything you do from now on within the profession.

In Chapter 1 we explore the Four Primary Motivators which make for effective training and communication. Executives and employees connect to compliance only when it becomes personal to them, and when it connects to their values. As explained in detail in this chapter, in my experience people are moved by one of four Primary Motivators: (1) Fear for Self, (2) Fear for the Business, (3) Noble Cause and (4) Competitive Edge.

Once you understand the Four Primary Motivators, specific techniques are described so that you can invoke each of them during training and meetings. Most importantly, you will be taught to recognize and record which Primary Motivator is most effective with each decision maker (or Power Source), so that you can become more effective over time with the person or people you must influence.

Next, you'll take the Company Neediness and Readiness Quiz to determine the best approach to use with your company and its executives, based on the intersection of (1) the company's readiness to change, and (2) the company's need for change. Armed with this knowledge, you'll be able to use the Compliance Officer Risk Matrix to determine your best approach with the company at which you work.

You'll then learn how to shine with management so that you're seen as a leader and a business asset. This chapter includes techniques to help you demonstrate your leadership and the ability to meet your goals and objectives in the eyes of the business.

Chapters 5 helps you to connect as a friend with the business. You will learn simple but extremely effective techniques to gain the trust of the business, so that you can become an indispensable member of the team. Special attention is paid in this chapter to winning over business people in foreign jurisdictions. For many compliance officers, becoming "one of the gang" can be incredibly challenging. This chapter explains concrete ways of becoming more likeable, and winning friends in a hurry.

"Hear and Be Heard" (Chapter 6) explores the sales techniques of David Sandler, who advocates mastery in listening in order to dramatically increase the efficacy of the salesperson. This chapter explains how to listen to influence others, how to know when to stop talking, and how to use words to make business leaders feel understood.

Chapters 8 and 9 turn to the topic of becoming known as an expert, both with immediate peers and within the field as a whole. Lastly, Chapter 10 helps you to deal with the hard stuff – rejection, defeat, criticism, and regulatory failure.

After reading "How to Be a Wildly Effective Compliance Officer," you will have new insights, skills, and techniques to become infinitely more effective at your job. You will be able to succeed in ways you have not been able to before, no matter how great your technical skillset or background. Being successful as a compliance officer is ultimately about gaining the trust of the business, and gaining trust occurs on an emotional level through persuasion, connection, and effective communication.

My Compliance Story

Over the past decade, I've been involved in some of the largest and most interesting compliance investigations and monitorships in the world. But I didn't start there. I began my career wanting to be an actress and producer in Hollywood. At 18, I left the cold confines of upstate New York to head to Hollywood to attend UCLA's School of Theater, Film and Television.

After graduating, I got a job at Paramount Pictures, working as an administrative assistant to the executives developing screenplays into movies. It was fascinating, but I was looking for a more dynamic environment than an office could provide. I left Paramount and worked in television production, working on programs for Fox FX Television and Sony TV. After a couple of years in film and TV, my goals changed and I decided to go to law school. I toiled my way through Loyola Law in Los Angeles, working full time during the day as a legal secretary, then going to school at night. After graduation, I joined the international law firm of Gibson, Dunn & Crutcher, working in their Los Angeles office and specializing in anti-bribery investigations and litigation.

Early in my legal career, I worked on the monitorship of the Siemens Corporation, which had been stung with the largest bribery fine in history, as well as the monitorship of a major pharmaceutical company. In 2011, Gibson Dunn sent me to London to work on an internal investigation of one of the banks caught up in a competition and rate-fixing scandal. I was supposed to stay only two years, but I fell in love, married a wonderful British man, and decided to stay in London. After nearly six years at Gibson Dunn, I left to become the Director of Compliance for Europe, the Middle East and Africa for the world's largest business travel company, Carlson Wagonlit Travel. There I was in charge of compliance in nearly 100 countries.

Ultimately, the siren song of entertainment called me back. I became the Chief Compliance Officer for United International Pictures, the joint international distribution company of Paramount Pictures and Universal Pictures. As the first full-time compliance professional at United International Pictures, it was my job to create a compliance program. I ran compliance for 60+ countries on four continents. As I travelled the world to perform training, I was inspired by the commitment of the people in the company to compliance and ethics.

In 2016, I began Spark Compliance Consulting, a boutique firm specializing in creating, implementing and optimizing compliance programs for multi-national companies. Spark focuses on revitalizing and restructuring compliance programs for corporations currently undergoing regulatory investigations, or that have experienced significant compliance failures in the past. Spark also specializes in helping companies establish and maintain compliance with European data privacy laws.

In addition to my job at Spark Compliance, I am an Adjunct Professor at Widener University Delaware School of Law, teaching Global Compliance and Ethics to their masters of jurisprudence students. It is an honor to teach practicing and budding compliance specialists about international laws, and how to be Wildly Effective compliance officers in a multinational environment.

Along the way I've been nominated for awards, including a nomination as part of Gibson Dunn for Best Regulatory Law Firm of the Year from Thomson Reuters in London, and Chief Compliance Officer of the Year at the Women in Compliance Awards.

I have delivered employee training in more than thirty-five countries on five continents, performed countless international internal investigations, and researched the laws in more countries than I can name. I have implemented compliance programs in places where none existed, and strengthened compliance programs where a complete breakdown had created chaos and public punishment of the company.

I've been speaking on compliance issues for years now, in England, the United States and throughout Europe. I've published articles in Legal Week Magazine, Compliance and Ethics Professional Magazine, and in trade publications. After more than a decade of getting it right (and sometimes getting it woefully wrong), I'm pleased to let you in on the secrets and strategies that will make you a Wildly Effective compliance officer. I know these techniques work because I have been using them and watching others use them for years.

Are You Ready?

Are you ready to be more effective than you ever thought possible? I thought so. Let's go!

Chapter 1: The Secret to Your Success — Using the Four Primary Motivators

A dark chill falls over the city, and no stars can be seen. In an unilluminated corner, steam wafts through the vents in the street, creating a foggy haze where evil seems to gather and lurk.

Out of the shadows comes a lone figure, donning a metaphorical cape, ready to protect the company. She is powerful, determined and focused.

She is a compliance officer.

OK, so it may seem that a compliance officer is an unlikely superhero by Hollywood standards, but stick with me, because if you are a compliance officer, you are in fact a superhero. Your job is to perform superhero tasks. You are charged with protecting your company from harm, investigating disturbances, uncovering plots against the company, punishing wrongdoers, and implementing measures to ensure the problems don't happen again. You keep the peace with your presence, and let the bad guys know you are watching for them. The fact that you exist creates fear in the hearts of would-be criminals. They are less likely to attempt their dastardly deeds because they know that you are in charge.

Part of a Movement Changing the World

Superman knows his mission is to fight a never-ending battle for truth and justice. Mighty Mouse sang, "Here I come to save the day!" You too must know your mission. You must believe in your cause and know you will succeed. You must have a vision.

For me, I view what I'm doing as changing the world. "Oh sure!" says the critic. "You work for a company in the compliance office! It's not exactly being the president of a country, or running an NGO dedicated to saving the environment!" No, but I'm on a mission.

The way I see it, corporate compliance is a movement, thrusting companies toward correct actions, a more ethical culture, and fairness. When compliance professionals perform anti-bribery training, they are making a difference in the world by explaining the laws to people, and making them aware of the red flags to alert them when a bribe is paid or being requested. I've been lucky enough to train employees in more than thirty-five countries. If just one person was affected in each training session, and sensitized to the effects of bribery within society, then I've helped to change the world.

Imagine how great the reach of the compliance movement is when compliance officers in thousands of companies perform training. Consider how quickly the world becomes a more transparent and fair place when multi-national companies decide it is more expensive and riskier to engage in bribery, or to collude or violate trade sanctions, than it is to do the job properly and ethically. Think of how many people will be affected because they are able to negotiate fairly with government contractors, or be paid a living wage, because bribes are not considered part of their compensation structure.

Remember that the anti-money laundering laws of the world are meant to stop criminal organizations, gangs, terrorism, and violence. Sometimes your job as a compliance officer may feel mundane, but don't lose heart! When you're checking to see if the Know Your Customer laws are being followed, you're really keeping the world safer by stopping the flow of ill-gotten gains to people committing crimes.

When things are going badly at work, remember that your mission is far bigger than the company for which you work. As long as you are training, teaching, implementing procedures, following up on audit reports, and responding to whistle-blower complaints, you are a person on a mission to make the world a better place.

The Power of Belief in Your Product

The first thing you need to know is that you're not *really* in compliance at all. You're in sales. What? No, really, you are in the business of selling compliance. You are selling your program every day to a wide audience. You're selling your vision of the future of the company, along with the tools that will help you to create that vision.

Zig Ziglar was an evangelistic believer in good salesmanship. In "Secrets of Closing the Sale," Ziglar states he believes anyone can sell anything, as long as they have a genuine belief in their product. Drawing from his own experience, Ziglar describes how he once worked as a door-to-door salesman of pots and pans. He believed so strongly in the quality of his pots and pans that he was totally convinced anyone who bought the pots and pans would be able to benefit from them for years to come. He visualized many wonderful meals the customers would be able to cook using the fabulous sauté pan. The pots and pans became a symbol to Ziglar of family events and healthy living, and he was able to sell the product effectively because he knew *he was giving the person buying the product more than the cost of the product.* He was giving the prospect the opportunity to benefit tremendously from what he was offering. His job, as he saw it, was to help the prospect see the benefits of the product, and to help them help themselves by choosing to purchase.

You may not think you have a product to sell, but you do. Your compliance program is your product. In order to effectively sell anything, you must fundamentally believe in your product. You must fully know the benefits of the product, and be able to describe them effectively – and in an emotionally engaging way.

The key question to answer is, *do you really, fundamentally believe in your product?* More accurately, perhaps the better question to ask is not, "Do you really, fundamentally believe in your product as it is now?" but rather, "Imagine your program as it could be. Do you really, fundamentally believe in your product as it would be if you had the resources and buy-in you need?" Yes? YES!

Ziglar laid out five powerful questions whose answers exemplify your belief in your product *as it could be.* Answer each one honestly:

1. Do you sell a pretty good product?
2. Do you sell an exceptionally good product?
3. Do you sell a product that solves a problem or problems?
4. Do you feel you should be appreciated and paid when you sell a product that solves a problem or problems?
5. Does the product that you sell solve a problem immediately, and then keeps solving the problem long after you've finished the sale?

Did you answer YES to each of these questions? I bet you did. Your program or product, if you could develop it sufficiently, would absolutely be an exceptionally good product. Your program would solve incredibly large problems. Your program would help avoid multi-million (or billion) dollar fines, keep people employed, protect the company and individuals from reputational damage, and secure the future of the business.

In Ziglar's book, he asks the reader to imagine a scenario in which the salesperson successfully sells a really good set of kitchen knives. Ziglar asks how long it will take the salesperson to spend the commission s/he made on the knives. One month? One week? OK, but how long does a really good set of kitchen knives last? Several years? A decade? Ziglar points out that the salesperson's income is short-lived, but the *value of the product* lasts much longer. Therefore, *the buyer gains the real value, not the salesperson.* The salesperson is therefore doing a favor for the person who buys the product by offering it in the first place.

This logic is fundamentally true regarding your compliance program as well. The value you provide in setting up a good program is much greater than your salary. You are providing an infrastructure that may long outlast your tenure at the company. If done correctly, your contributions may last longer than you live on this planet! You are providing something of enormous value in your product.

You are offering an exceptionally good product that solves problems and will be around long after the initial investment is made. Your belief must be unshakable. When you believe in your product, you can sell it.

So, the first step is to genuinely believe in, and be committed to, what you are selling. The next step is to engage your internal business associates so that they become believers as well, and they emotionally connect with your vision. I am convinced that you can't be Wildly Effective at this job without implementing techniques that elicit the emotional buy-in of your internal audience.

But how do you obtain emotional buy-in? I have found that everyone emotionally relates to at least one of the Four Primary Motivators. Used correctly, these motivators can increase tremendously the buy-in for your program, and create rapport between you and your internal audience. The Four Primary Motivators are referenced throughout this book. Understand these, and you will increase your effectiveness remarkably.

The Four Primary Motivators

The Four Primary Motivators are:
- Fear for Self
- Fear for the Business
- Noble Cause
- Competitive Edge

Fear for Self

Fear for Self centers on the avoidance of personal pain or difficulty. Former Assistant Attorney General for the Criminal Division of the Department of Justice Lanny Breuer told the truth when he said, "The strongest deterrent against corporate crime is the prospect of prison time for individual employees."[6]

> "The strongest deterrent against corporate crime is the prospect of prison time for individual employees." – Lanny Breuer

Most people in the corporate world consider themselves unlikely to be involved in criminality. They think big fines happen to someone else, and even if the company is fined, nothing will happen to them. It's time to wake these people up!

Many people are primarily motivated by Fear for Self. The science of persuasion tells us that people are most affected by stories of individuals *most similar to themselves.*[7] Therefore, when dealing with those motivated by Fear for Self, it is critical to engage them using stories of someone similar to themselves. Whenever possible, use a story of someone of the same age, gender, position in the company (manager, regular employee, board member, etc.), or in the same industry. Tell real and specific stories that bring home the risk to the individual. Use big number fines and trends in jail time — which always seem to be increasing, not decreasing — to intensify the impact of your stories. I maintain a list of resources for the compliance professional on www.ComplianceKristy.com that will help you to find statistics and stories that you can use.

Here's an important tip: Deliberately look people in the eye during training when you talk to them about the potential of imprisonment. Make the threat real and personal. Employees are much more focused on policies when they understand the personal cost of failure. Whenever I train outside the United States and the United Kingdom, I warn people that they can be personally extradited for trial and imprisonment in the U.S. or U.K. for violations of bribery and competition laws. For many, the shock is palpable. They didn't know that, but now that they do, they are will always be aware of the personal risk.

During my training sessions, I always make a point of reminding people that company money spent on fines, lawyers and investigations means less for raises and bonuses. People connect with compliance when they internalize that the answer to "What's in it for me?" is: (1) their job, (2) their freedom, and (3) their future at the organization.

Fear for the Business

The second Primary Motivator is Fear for the Business. This motivation centers on avoidance of problems in the business. Most business leaders love the business in which they work. Top executives, creators, owners and board members do not want to see the reputation of their company sullied by news reports of illegal conduct. More importantly, they don't want to slash the budget and their bonuses so they can pay huge fines to the government for corporate wrongdoing.

Like Fear for Self, people motivated by Fear for the Business are best reached by stories of businesses similar to the one in which they work. To be most effective, you will want to find stories of businesses in serious trouble that are related to your business. Search for stories about businesses in the same industry, country, service type or size as the business for which you work.

Fines can be very expensive, increasingly in the billions for serious violations. Fear for the Business can really be ramped up when you describe the multiple types of sanctions that can be applied. For instance, you can describe the difference between criminal fines and civil fines. You can also describe class action lawsuits and private plaintiff lawsuits. If you are in a publically-traded business, and your country allows share-holder derivative suits, you can explain the devastation a multi-year battle with your shareholders can cause.

You can also describe the knock-on effect many laws have if you have multi-national operations. For example, let's say your company operates in the U.S. and the U.K. You can increase your effectiveness by explaining that a bribe made entirely in another jurisdiction (for example, Japan) could cause the company to be prosecuted in the United States, the United Kingdom, and Japan. This knowledge can scare even the most hardened CEO.

In addition, if you work for a company that has government contracts, explaining that the company could be debarred or not allowed to bid on government contracts in the future can be a great incentive to create buy-in to the compliance program from the business.

Fear for the Business and Fear for Self work in much the same way, but touch different motivations. Many stories can be used for two purposes. If you have a story about a business in a similar industry that has gotten in trouble, dig deeper to try to find a story or two about individuals in the business who suffered at the same time as the company, with individual penalties. Stories like these emotionally connect to people with fear-based motivations, which can help you to be Wildly Effective when you present solutions to the problems faced by the company.

Noble Cause

This motivation centers on pride in corporate social responsibility, and in being the most ethical company possible. For some companies in the business community, connecting to the ideals of corporate social responsibility and ethical business is easy. Many companies, such as Starbucks or TOMS Shoes, use their ethical business credentials as a marketing element. For companies who are members of the United Nations Global Compact, corporate social responsibility is a mandate they have chosen to fund and measure.

If you are lucky enough to work for a company with corporate social responsibility or ethical business as part of its identity or marketing, congratulations! Things may be easier for you, as you sell compliance as part of the corporate mission. A company with an espoused ethos of positive governance is much more likely to be compelled to protect its reputation, and the reputations of its employees, by complying with all laws and regulations.

Likewise, you may be lucky enough to work with individuals or business leaders who hold themselves to high ethical standards, and believe that complying with the law is simply the right thing to do. If you are employed in a company or with people who are motivated by Noble Cause, you should work to inspire them to be their best selves when it comes to complying with the law, and to instill in them the sense of purpose you connect to as being part of the movement of compliance that can and is changing the world.

People motivated by Noble Cause will respond most strongly to stories where the company is put in the spotlight as one to emulate and admire. Compliance professionals should focus on finding storylines where the business is seen to be doing more for the world, or being at the forefront of the most ethical business within the industry, country or environment in which the business operates. People motivated by Noble Cause like to imagine their company is a shining beacon on the hill. They want their company to be the benchmark against which other companies compare themselves. Use this motivator to show them how much better the company could be with continued compliance investment and improvement.

Competitive Edge

The Primary Motivator of Competitive Edge centers on winning business through the use of compliance as a business advantage. Many sales people can be lured onto the side of compliance when motivated by winning business through the use of Competitive Edge.

Compliance, good governance and proper procedures really can be a business advantage. If there hasn't yet been a scandal in your industry or region of the world, there will be eventually. Because multi-national corporations are frequently the ones concerned with compliance and procedures, you can tell your business units that ethical business and a good compliance program is the best way to position your business to win large contracts.

Additionally, world governments are more and more frequently requiring compliance programs and supply chain compliance as part of their criteria for awarding contracts. In the United States, for instance, government contracts must have compliance provisions throughout the supply chain to ensure that no forced labor is utilized. If a company has a powerful compliance program in place, new regulations are less likely to disrupt business.

In order to effectively use Competitive Edge, you should tell stories of similar companies in your industry or aligned industries that won contracts or business because of the strength of their compliance program. For example, I was fortunate enough to be at Carlson Wagonlit Travel when the GlaxoSmithKline scandal struck. Allegedly, GlaxoSmithKline had been moving money through travel agencies in China in order to create a slush fund that could be used to pay bribes to doctors in China to prescribe their drugs. All of a sudden the major multi-national pharmaceutical companies were banging on the door at Carlson Wagonlit Travel, as it had not been associated with the travel agencies alleged to have been involved in the scandal in China. Carlson Wagonlit Travel's compliance program, membership in the United Nations Global Compact, membership in TRACE International, and reputation for responsible business was a major business advantage. Those memberships and programs, which had occasionally been questioned by various people within the business, suddenly became marketing and sales tools the business could exploit for greater sales.

Using the Four Primary Motivators to Be Wildly Effective

Now that you know and understand the Four Primary Motivators, you can use them to make your training much more effective. Throughout every company there are people with different Primary Motivators. To be most effective, you should include stories and examples relating to every Primary Motivator in any training session that you do. By using every Motivator, you can reach every audience member in a deep, emotional way.

To be most effective, you should include stories and examples relating to every Primary Motivator in any training session that you do. By using every Motivator, you will reach every audience member in a deep emotional way.

To intensify the effectiveness of the Four Primary Motivators, you must be able to use them with specificity with each Power Source at your company. The next chapter will show you how to use your knowledge of the Four Primary Motivators to make yourself even more effective with the leaders of your organization.

For a free downloadable template in which you can plan your training to include stories relating to each Primary Motivator, visit www.ComplianceKristy.com. There you will also find example templates relating to several industries to help you make your training Wildly Effective.

Chapter 2: Plugging Into the Power Sources

"When Kristy first came to work here, I thought, what on Earth is she going to do all day? But now, compliance is a part of our daily lives, and I cannot imagine what we ever did without her." That email was sent from the President of my region to all of the country managers the day I left my job. I had made myself indispensable to the business by using the Four Primary Motivators to connect to the Power Sources.

I've seen compliance officer after compliance officer fail miserably at their job when they don't connect properly to the Power Sources. Everyone goes into the job knowing that they need to win over the business. But how is this done in practice? And more importantly, how does one go from being connected to the Power Sources to becoming indispensable to the business?

Let's face it — most people in the business don't know what the Compliance Department does, nor do they really want to know. What they do know is that the Compliance Officer (you) have what my husband calls, "the power of smite." The compliance officer can block projects. The compliance officer can stop new initiatives and sales schemes. The compliance officer can suss out wrongdoing and recommend punishments and terminations. The compliance officer is scary.

Fear may help you control the business, but to become really indispensable, you must show the business your vision, and get them to buy into it.

Chapter 1 delineated the Four Primary Motivators that inspire business action toward compliant behavior. The Four Primary Motivators are (1) Fear for Self, (2) Fear for the Business, (3) Noble Cause and (4) Competitive Edge. In this chapter, you will learn to utilize these Four Primary Motivators to connect to the Power Sources. Your job is to implement a two-part plan: Part One is to understand the Primary Motivation of the Power Sources. Part Two is to utilize these Motivators to go beyond the initial conversation and convert each Power Source to a believer in your highest vision for the company.

Identifying the Power Sources

In every business, family, group of friends, or club there are two sources of power — the named power and the covert power. The named power is the obvious source of authority. In business, the named power is almost always the manager, President or CEO and the members of the Board of Directors.

The second source of power is the covert power. Covert power tends to come from people who are highly charismatic, well-connected, or long-established within the company. Whenever you're in a room with the business managers, look around to see who has covert power. You can usually determine this by observing the responses of the listeners to the person who is talking. The comments of some people are quickly dismissed or ignored, while those of others are carefully considered. You can also determine who has covert power by noting the people who are consistently chosen to lead important projects.

People with covert power are incredibly important resources. If you are able to connect with those with covert power so that they become compliance believers, you will have a much better likelihood of success.

Ideally, you want to connect with, and obtain buy-in from, both the people with named power and covert power. People with covert power who believe in your compliance mission will carry compliance ideas into their meetings and processes. Since they are natural leaders, others will follow their lead.

If possible, you should establish your role so that you have a direct line of reporting to the top Power Sources, usually including both the CEO and the Board of Directors. Your direct access will allow you to perform your job at the highest possible level, without interference or screening by the business or the General Counsel.

Leveraging the Primary Motivator with the Power Sources

Each company will have a dominant Primary Motivator, and each individual within a company will also have a Primary Motivator. Companies tend to attract people with similar Primary Motivators. To be most effective, you must leverage both the Primary Motivator of the company and the Primary Motivator of each individual Power Source.

Finding the Primary Motivator of the Business

You can determine the Primary Motivator of the business by looking at how the company portrays itself in its marketing. View the company's website. Does the company promote its ethical credentials and sustainable business objectives? If so, your company probably has an overriding Primary Motivator of Noble Cause. If your company's press releases are dominated by sales figures and descriptions of how they beat the competition, your company's Primary Motivator is probably Competitive Edge.

A company's choice of values can also give a strong indication of the Primary Motivator of the business. Does the company espouse collaboration and integrity as its values? Or does it value cutting-edge technology and maintaining shareholder profitability?

Another way to determine the Primary Motivator of your company is to review what they publish or write, both in internal and external communications. What is the story behind your company? What is the story the company is trying to sell? Some companies position themselves as the most ecological in the business, or the most "green." Companies with this sensibility are more likely to have Power Sources that respond to Noble Cause as their Primary Motivator.

Once you've determined which Primary Motivator applies to the business, you will know which Primary Motivator to favor in your training. Because people tend to join a company that speaks to their own personal values and motivations, the Primary Motivator of the company is likely to be reflected in the majority of the people working at the company.

To get to the next level, however, you'll need to reach each Power Source individually with their individual Primary Motivator.

Finding the Primary Motivator of Each Power Source

In order to be Wildly Effective, your first job is to determine which of the Four Primary Motivators is the strongest for each Power Source. The President of the company may have a different Primary Motivator than the members of the Board. Although many boards have a group Primary Motivator, if you are able to spend time with each member of the Board, you may find that each has a different Primary Motivator.

So, how do you figure out the Primary Motivator for each Power Source? The first way is to watch carefully during your training to see which slides or stories seem to have the greatest effect on each Power Source. Some Power Sources visibly wince when stories are told of executives being indicted, or extradited to face trial. Others will become engaged when you speak of Competitive Edge in your training. A primary reason to include slides with all Four Primary Motivators in your training is so that you can study the Power Sources to see what they respond to.

Watch carefully when you tell stories of executives going to jail or losing their jobs during your training. Does the leader fidget, look down, sigh, or roll his or her eyes? As more and more compliance investigations and scandals strip executives of their jobs, more executives are motivated by Fear for Self. Ten years ago, it was relatively unheard of for an executive to receive anything other than a slap on the wrist for malfeasance. This is no longer true. In a world where the United States and United Kingdom are extraditing executives for bribery and competition violations, executives are more and more aware of the perils of compliance failures. Indeed, the boards of many organizations fire leaders who have been complicit in compliance failures. Fear for Self can be a major motivator to get the leader to buy into your vision.

I was training in Denmark a couple of years back, and it was clear to me that the company leader's Primary Motivator was Fear for Self. I determined this because during training, the leader was clearly taken aback by stories of executives being sent to jail. She whispered, "Oh, my gosh!" and reacted strongly when being told of other companies whose compliance failures had caused the downfall of prominent people in the industry.

When I met privately with this Power Source to discuss the compliance program, I expressed my gratitude for her careful attention during the training. I told her that I was there to *make sure nothing like that would ever happen to her.* I then explained the plan to make sure *that nothing like that ever happened to her.* At this point, she was relieved to buy into compliance, as I was offering a solution to her problem. She may not have known of her risks before training, but now that the training had finished, she knew she could experience severe consequences if she did not properly manage the company's business. She was therefore compelled to learn how she could protect herself, and compliance had the answers she needed.

My former colleague Angelika was in charge of compliance for a prominent university in the United States. She reported to the Board of Trustees and she quickly determined that the Board as a whole had Noble Cause as their Primary Motivator. As she delivered the training, she spoke in glowing terms of the *respect the University would receive* by virtue of its world-class compliance program. She sold the Board on her vision of a *better world* where students enjoyed talking about the ethical environment of the institute. The Board related to the vision of the university as the leading institution in the field, and was excited to move forward with her compliance program. She had properly tapped into the Motivator of the Power Sources, and thereafter received the support she needed for increased resources and more autonomy.

In contrast, choosing the wrong Motivator for a Power Source can be a recipe for disaster. If you are dealing with a Power Source motivated by Competitive Edge, trying to use Fear for Self may make the Power Source feel accused of wrongdoing, or defensive. If the Power Source becomes defensive, it is almost impossible to get the buy-in required to be a Wildly Effective compliance officer. Likewise, if you use Noble Cause with a Power Source who is motivated by Fear for the Business, you will likely lose your audience, as he or she will think you are out of touch with the business realities faced in this "tough economic climate" (and it's always a tough economic climate).

Rolando was a compliance officer who truly believed doing business ethically was imperative, and that his company could be set apart with public accolades for the responsible business initiatives he wanted to implement. He noticed that the covert Power Source, the Vice President of Development, seemed frustrated with the responsible business initiative that he was trying to launch, and he asked her what he could do to help her team. She responded that she thought responsible business was fine, but it didn't help her bottom line. As a result of that conversation, Rolando was able to determine that Competitive Edge was this Power Source's Primary Motivator.

Rolando subsequently went to her with a plan to boost sales by showing how the compliance elements of the responsible business plan could be a major selling point. In Rolando's industry there was a third-party rating company that gave awards based on ethical business. Rolando convinced the Vice President that more business would come their way as a result of these awards and accolades. Rolando was speaking this woman's language. She bought into the compliance program because Rolando used her Primary Motivator to make her feel that these initiatives would benefit her directly.

What if Rolando had continued to use Noble Cause to try and motivate the Vice President? It is unlikely that the Vice President would ever have responded as Rolando hoped. She would likely have been polite, but would not have bought in the way she did when he went to her with a sales pitch that worked with her Primary Motivator.

Putting it Together

Once you've discovered the business' Primary Motivator and each Power Source's Primary Motivator, you can tailor your training and conversations to emotionally connect to the individual. As you'll find out throughout the remainder of the book, emotional connection is critical to making you indispensable to the business, and to being Wildly Effective. The next step is to learn how to approach the business based on its need for change and its readiness for change.

Chapter 3: Use the Wildly Effective Compliance Officer Risk Matrix to Super-Charge Your Approach

Congratulations, Compliance Officer – you got the job, or you're in the job! The trouble is, you can't do this job effectively by yourself. You must have the buy-in of the business. What is buy-in? Buy-in means that the Power Sources in the business believe in your mission and support your mandate. The level of buy-in from the business will frequently determine whether you are able to be effective in your job, or not. Obtaining the buy-in of the business is what this chapter is all about. Read on to find out how to get buy-in at the highest levels, so you can be Wildly Effective at your job.

Using the Wildly Effective Compliance Officer Risk Matrix

Compliance and risk officers love a good risk matrix. A properly done risk matrix measures the risk of having a compliance failure. It's usually based on a combination of how likely a failure is to happen, and how much damage a failure could cause. A risk matrix gives the Compliance Officer a good idea of how to respond to the multiple risks facing the company, and helps the company to prioritize its use of limited resources.

Choosing the proper approach for your company is a crucial matter. How you choose to approach the business will determine whether or not you get the buy-in you need from the business. To determine what approach to use, Wildly Effective compliance officers use the Wildly Effective Compliance Officer Matrix.

One axis of the Matrix represents how much change the company needs. The other axis represents how ready the company is for change. The place of intersection represents the best approach for implementing your program.

You may intuitively know where your company is on the chart, or you may have no idea. To determine your best approach, answer the following questions, and then tally up your score.

Quiz: How Ready is Your Organization for Change?

Add up the number of times you choose the A or B answers to the following questions.

1.) Has the CEO, President, or Board announced publically that compliance is a priority at the company, or publically endorsed the importance of the changes that are coming because of the compliance program?

A. Yes ___

B. No ___

2.) Were you hired or promoted with specific instructions to implement one or more aspects of the compliance program? For example, were you hired with the understanding that you would implement a whistle-blower hotline immediately?

A. Yes ___

B. No ___

3.) Does the company already have a functioning compliance program?

A. Yes ___

B. No ___

4.) Does your company shy away from change?

A. No ___

B. Yes ___

5.) Do you feel like you spend half of your time explaining what a compliance program is to people who don't understand and don't want to understand?

A. No ___

B. Yes ___

Add up the points from your A and B scores.

Number of A: _____

Number of B: _____

If the A points outnumber the B points, your organization has a High Readiness for Change. If your B points outnumber your A points, your organization has a Low Readiness for Change.

Based on your score, enter whether your company has a High or Low Readiness for Change here: _____

Quiz: How Much Need is there for Change in Your Organization?

Add up the number of times you choose the A or B answers to the following questions.

1.) Has your company recently been fined, prosecuted, or found guilty of a compliance violation?

A. Yes ____

B. No ____

2.) Has your company recently been put under investigation for a compliance violation?

A. Yes ____

B. No ____

3.) Has your industry recently been under scrutiny from the authorities?

A. Yes ____

B. No ____

4.) Have one or more of your competitors recently been fined, prosecuted, put under investigation or found guilty of a compliance violation?

A. Yes ___
B. No ___

5.)   Has anyone in senior management at your company been fired in the past year (publically or not) for compliance violations?
A. Yes ___
B. No ___

Add up the points from your A and B scores.
    Number of A: _____
    Number of B: _____

If the A points outnumber the B points, your organization has a High Need for Change. If the B points outnumber the A points, your organization has a Low Need for Change.

Based on your score, enter whether your company has a High or Low Need for Change here: _____

Next, enter your scores from the Readiness to Change section and the Need for Change section in the appropriate boxes, and then see which quadrant your company falls into on the Wildly Effective Compliance Officer Matrix. Let's look at each quadrant to see how a Wildly Effective Compliance Officer should approach his or her job.

Wildly Effective Compliance Officer
Risk Matrix

Readiness for Change

HIGH

High Readiness
Low Need

High Readiness
High Need

Low Readiness
Low Need

Low Readiness
High Need

LOW

Need for Change

HIGH

Low Readiness/Low Need

Companies in this quadrant have a low readiness for change. The good news is that they also have a low need for change, which means your approach should be slow and steady. These companies often have highly functioning compliance programs already in place. It could be that your industry experienced compliance failures in the past, either through regulation or prosecution, and already required good compliance programs. It could also be that your company had a trailblazing Wildly Effective compliance officer, and therefore your job is to continue the program that has already been created, while responding to new regulatory developments.

If you are working at a Low Readiness/Low Need company, your first job is to understand what is already working. When you perform your risk analysis, carefully observe who the compliance champions are within the business. Be sure to make friends with people who have already bought-in to the need for compliance, and who think that the compliance officer can be a friend and helper.

When you begin to introduce change at a Low Readiness/Low Need company, do so slowly, perhaps by shifting the focus of the current program, or by instituting more bells and whistles to already established program elements. For example, you could expand the advertising and awareness campaign for the whistle-blower hotline by putting the local toll-free number on the payment stubs of all of the employees one month. Or perhaps you can get the CEO to tape a one-minute introduction to this year's online anti-bribery training. Whatever you do, you can take the program and slowly make it bigger and better.

Low Readiness/Low Need companies provide great places to hone best practices, and to work at a place you will likely be proud of for having a good program. However, these environments can sometimes be boring when it feels like there is nothing new to create. Don't worry too much if this is the case for you, as an internal investigation or new regulation will arrive soon enough, which will see you evaluating the program to help it evolve to mitigate new risks.

Low Readiness/High Need

Companies in this quadrant have a high need for change, but a low readiness to embrace the change they need. This is the most dangerous quadrant for a compliance officer, as the compliance officer can see the flashing red lights, but no one else at the company seems to sense the danger.

Many companies fall into this quadrant. Companies here tend to be in high-risk industries that have not yet become aware of the changes required to comply with best practices being implemented by other companies. Often companies in this quadrant are aware that their competitors are being investigated, but they have not grasped that the investigation may bleed over from the competitors to them. For example, if the Department of Justice in the U.S. is doing one of its famous "industry sweeps," but your company hasn't received a letter of inquiry yet, it may still think it is safe.

If you are in a Low Readiness/High Need company, you need to evaluate two things: (1) What is already working that can be leveraged; and (2) What immediate steps will be tolerated by the business, while you work on selling the rest of what you know needs to happen to protect the company?

Let's look at an example. Ingleterre Industries is an international importer of cotton to Europe. It competes with two other importation companies, one of which has been named in an investigation for using forced labor on farms in Uzbekistan. Ingleterre works with farmers in Uzbekistan to obtain cotton, but it is sure that the farmers they use are good guys, as they pay a living wage to their workers and have compliance obligations in their contracts. However, Ingleterre has never performed any supply chain audit, nor does it have any due diligence process in place for choosing suppliers.

When Sheila was hired as the new compliance officer at Ingleterre, she immediately wanted to implement a supply chain audit and a due diligence system that vets all suppliers before they can be used. However, she knew from discussions during her interviews that this level of immediate change would be perceived as chaotic to the business, and she did not want to be marginalized as "anti-business." Instead, Sheila first leveraged what was working well. Sheila saw that the contracts included compliance obligations, but they did not yet include audit rights or indemnifications. Therefore, she beefed up the compliance obligations with the help of the legal department, and then asked the business to implement the new compliance obligations in the form of contract amendments with the suppliers. The new contract amendments included explicit reference to Ingleterre's Code of Conduct, which the suppliers were required to abide by.

As the new amendments were rolled out, Sheila began to work with the business unit in charge of the highest-risk suppliers. When the media published accounts of forced labor being used by her competitors, she performed an internal investigation to ensure that Ingleterre wasn't using those suppliers.

Sheila began to talk to the business about due diligence and performing "spot checks." She described the audit as a way to protect the company, and convinced the business that due diligence was both necessary and critical. This took several months. Once the reputational damage began to effect the competitor companies, Sheila re-doubled her efforts, and convinced the business to implement a full-blown due diligence system to ensure that Ingleterre was protected.

Sheila was successful because she did not try to shock the business immediately with all of the things she wanted to do. Instead, she leveraged what was already working well to make it work better, and then implemented the protections that were crucial to the company. Lastly, she began to work her ideas into conversations about proper supply chain audits and due diligence, knowing that these will protect the company in the long run.

Low Readiness/High Need companies can be difficult places to work. However, with the proper skillset and approach, these companies can become beacons of compliance and ethics.

High Readiness/Low Need

Companies in this quadrant have a high readiness for change but a low need. These companies have frequently been through a prosecution or compliance crisis and have implemented a compliance program, but still don't feel like they are truly protected. Sometimes a very ethical executive has come into the company to lead it, and he or she is demanding the very best program, where a pretty good program already exits. If you are in a company in the High Readiness/Low Need category, you are likely to be in a position to be very effective.

Ralph joined a High Readiness/Low Need company last year. The company was a law firm that hired him to be their compliance officer. Because the law firm had good management, they had already implemented good practices in relation to their anti-money laundering, fraud prevention, and record retention risk. However, the company lacked a formal compliance program until Ralph took over. Ralph was concerned that he wouldn't appear to be doing "enough" to justify the cost of hiring him.

The first thing Ralph did was to brand the compliance function. He added the words "Compliance and Ethics" in a special font to the firm's logo, which he used as his branding any time the Compliance Department sent out an email. He also used the branding on his slides when he performed training at the firm. In this way, Ralph formalized the compliance program to highlight the areas that he was responsible for within the firm.

Ralph also leveraged the good practices already in place in the firm by codifying them into written procedures. In this way, he knew that if there were ever an investigation or something went wrong, he would be able to rely on his program's structure. Ralph's job wasn't to re-invent the wheel. He simply needed to create an identity for compliance, and to codify and formalize the good practices that already existed at the firm.

High Readiness/High Need

Companies in this quadrant have a high readiness for change, and a high need for change. If this describes your company, congratulations — you likely took a very exciting job! Perhaps you came to the company just after a compliance meltdown created fines or tremendous reputational damage. Perhaps you're dealing with a corporate monitor assigned by a judge or regulator, so you have to impose a new program in order to please the government or to fulfill your Deferred or Non-Prosecution Agreement. Or perhaps someone has uncovered a large-scale fraud, bribery scheme, or collusion at the company. Shock and awe, and the need for speed, is upon you.

The good news about working in a High Readiness/High Need company is that you are likely to have both the resources and the goodwill to change the system, and to implement the programs needed. There is a famous quote within the compliance community: "Never waste a good crisis." If the company has experienced crisis or compliance failure, the business will expect you to implement swift and striking changes.

You should come in with a clear agenda and a vision for how to fix the problems, and demand that the business partner with you to implement the changes. You are likely in an excellent position to make a big difference at the company. It may, however, be a bumpy ride.

When I was in private practice, I served on multiple teams performing corporate monitorships. A monitor is often assigned to a company as part of a plea bargain or a negotiated settlement with the government when the company has committed widespread malfeasance. One of my assignments involved the monitorship of Siemens, which had been punished with the largest fine in corporate history for bribery ($1.6 billion dollars). The monitor and his counsel were assigned the multi-year task of revamping Siemens' compliance program, auditing the program, and making the changes necessary to convince the United States' and German governments that Siemens had changed.

As part of the monitorship, I interviewed executives in Germany and Mexico, and worked on revamping the program in Argentina. Our team broke down the silos that had existed within the company to establish a cohesive program. Ultimately, we had to fire people who would not accept that the new culture of compliance was here to stay.

A monitor can be a great motivator to ensure that the company complies, but it doesn't take a monitorship to put the company into a High Readiness/High Need situation. For the adrenaline junkie compliance officer, High Readiness/High Need scenarios provide the perfect opportunity to create the best compliance program that can exist at a company, as resources will be available and people will be paying attention to ensure that the culture of compliance takes hold.

What Now?

In addition to the general approach suggested by the Wildly Effective Compliance Officer Risk Matrix, you should use the other tools at your disposal in order to pinpoint exactly how to approach the company on a risk-by-risk basis. Perhaps overall your program is very good, but your competition or antitrust risks haven't been addressed properly. In that case, your overall response to the business may follow the Low Need / Low Readiness model, but with respect to competition issues, you may need to follow the High Need / Low Readiness approach. Additionally, if you have engagement surveys, culture surveys or other indications of readiness and need for change, you should incorporate those into your evaluation and response.

After you've successfully identified where your company is on the matrix, you need to show the Power Sources at your company that you shine, the topic of Chapter 4.

Chapter 4: Showing the Power Sources that You Shine

Once you've established the identities of the Power Sources (both formal and covert), how do you demonstrate your importance? One of the main problems with an effective compliance program is that nothing happens. It's the rare executive that says, "Congratulations Beth! We didn't have any fines or regulatory investigations this year. You must be doing an excellent job." No, more often than not, the more successful you are at deterring illegal and unethical activity, the easier it is for the business to believe they should de-invest in compliance because clearly they don't need to continue investing in the program.

Your challenge is to keep connected to the Power Sources in a way that shows your progress. Most business people (and especially accountants) love metrics. C-suite executives in particular love goals, bullet points, graphs, and progress reports. Measuring culture change isn't easy, but it can be done. One of your major challenges will be to display your achievements in a way that resonates with the Power Sources so you continue to be valued for the contributions you are making to the company.

The Best Way to Say "I'm Awesome!" Every Month

When I became the Chief Compliance Officer of United International Pictures, my direct line of reporting was to the Board and the COO. This was fantastic, but it was also a major shift for me. I went from having bosses who directly oversaw my work, to business leaders who weren't aware of my day-to-day wins and losses. My previous bosses had been invested in my growth. They gave me performance reviews and carefully watched to see how I was progressing. All of a sudden, the kudos and feedback were stripped out of my life. The Board and COO were busy, and not at all interested in talking to me on a daily basis about the progress of the creation, implementation, and management of the compliance program.

My dear friend in compliance at Rolls Royce suggested I create a Compliance Dashboard, which I was to send every month to the members of the Board and the C-suite at my company. The Compliance Dashboard was a single-sheet showing: (1) my annual goals in each area of the seven elements of a successful compliance program; and (2) my progress toward each goal. Here's a generic example of my Compliance Dashboard:

Compliance Dashboard – [Month and Year]		
Big Seven	**Annual Goals**	**Progress Update**
(1) Policies and Procedures	• Re-draft Anti-Bribery Policy	• New policy has been drafted, approved and implemented throughout the company.
(2) Training	• Perform in-person training in nine countries, including two in Europe and four in Asia based on the risk assessment	• Training completed in France and Germany. • Scheduled trips include Vietnam in October and Laos in November.
(3) Monitoring	• Launch Ethics Helpline throughout Europe	• Launch of Ethics Helpline complete in eighteen countries. • Launch awaited in seven others because we need European data protection authorities' approval before launching.
(4) Messaging	• Launch new Compliance section of the public-facing website	• Draft Compliance section of the public-facing website created. Awaiting final approval and roll-out globally.
(5) Due Diligence	• Implement Intermediary Management System • Draft procedures for risk analysis and due diligence	• Intermediary Management Contract signed and implementation complete. Roll-out ready to begin.
(6) Risk Assessment	• Complete annual risk assessment • Bring in outside consulting firm to review program and benchmark program against similarly sized companies in our industry	• Contacted Spark Compliance Consulting to request initial meeting regarding reviewing the program and benchmarking it against other similarly sized companies in our industry.
(7) Governance	• Create every-other-month calls with mini-committee	• Call scheduled for [Date] • Next full meeting [Date]

By sending out the monthly Compliance Dashboard, you give the business a way to be aware of and monitor your progress. You also give yourself the gift of benchmarking to see how far you've come each month toward completing your goals. The Compliance Dashboard provides an easy way to prove you are moving the program forward and adding value to the business.

If you haven't ever sent out a Compliance Dashboard, I recommend you create one and send it to the C-suite and/or Board of Directors with a note that you will be sending an updated copy each month. If anyone ever wonders what you do, you can show them clear progress on a monthly basis.

Annual Reviews and Metrics

Many companies insist each person and department have goals that are developed annually. However, not every company has such requirements. The last company at which I worked did not have annual reviews, and did not require annual goal-setting. I decided to create goals for the compliance program anyway. I shared them at the board meetings, and I obtained full buy-in for my three-year plan every year.

It is critically important to create an annual and a monthly plan. You need to know what to focus on, and having annual goals is a good way to ensure that the most important items are accomplished.

There have been many reports and studies done on the metrics being used by compliance officers to show the progression of the program. Some of these metrics include:

- Number of calls to the whistle-blower hotline and disposition of each issue
- Number of training hours completed on a per-employee basis
- Results of surveys regarding engagement, culture and awareness of the compliance program
- Number of compliance policies
- Number of investigations or regulatory requests responded to within the year
- Number of countries in which the whistle-blower hotline is operating
- Amount of money invested in compliance-related expenditure

The importance of each of these metrics is debatable, but you should measure the effectiveness of your program in at least a few ways, so that you can show how well you are doing and how much you have progressed since you began your job. Metrics make people feel confident that something is being accomplished. Use this to your advantage.

Keeping the Kudos for When You Need Them

When I was at Gibson Dunn, one of my favorite bosses kept a file on her computer called "Wins!" She created a new Word document each year. The document was divided into two sections. One section detailed all of the little wins she had throughout the year. In this section she would note when she won an argument in court, helped a client through a tough situation, or was mentioned in the press in her city. At the end of the year she would have a detailed record of all of her accomplishments, so she could present her value to the partnership in a detailed way.

The second part of the Wins! document was entitled "Praise." In this section she kept copies of emails from clients or counsel telling her she'd done a good job. Whenever she was feeling low or experienced a setback, she would go into her Wins! document and review her accomplishments and the praise she had garnered throughout the year.

I began keeping my own Wins! file several years ago. It has kept me on track when I've felt like I'm not able to be Wildly Effective. There is more on what to do when you're feeling down in Chapter 10, but in the meantime, begin collecting praise about yourself, and writing down your accomplishments as you go. When you get to the end of the year (or to your annual review), you'll easily be able to talk up your accomplishments with specific examples, so the Power Sources know you've been Wildly Effective. This one habit will change your life, as you'll easily be able to quantify the terrific job you've done (and why you should be remunerated accordingly).

Next we'll explore how to get close to the business so you become an ally. Being thought of as a trusted advisor and friend will help you to be Wildly Effective.

Chapter 5: Critical Bridges to the Business – Getting on the Inside Track

This is a true story. Only the names have been changed to protect the guilty.

Manager 1: We had a great time at our meeting in Paris. Kristy was out with us 'til one in the morning.

Manager 2: What? You mean the compliance officer?

Manager 1: Yeah, she's so much fun! You don't understand; she's awesome. She's one of us. You should invite her out. She's great.

Impossible? Nope. In my estimation, the biggest problem and the greatest gift you have is your title. The word "compliance" can evoke images of dominatrix characters, war criminals, or worse. "Compliance" is frequently associated with negative power, restriction of movement, and lack of freedom.

To become Wildly Effective, your job is to become a business asset. It's a big leap to go from "Dr. No" to being perceived as a critical and useful partner in the business. My favorite description of a compliance officer is "One who protects the business five years from now." In five years, the company's executives won't be worried about this quarter's profits. They won't be worried about this year's potential bonuses. They will be worried about long-term growth and success.

Getting them to Say, "You Don't Understand, Our Compliance Officer Is Awesome!"

I used to travel once a month to Paris from London to attend the Europe, Middle East and Africa management meetings of the company for which I worked. I was the first compliance officer for the company in my region. Because of the CEO's commitment to compliance, management was told that Compliance (aka: me) was to be invited to the monthly meetings. Although I don't know for sure, I can speculate with some certainty that the first thought of the regular management attendees wasn't, "YES! Compliance is coming to our two-day meetings!" No, I'm pretty sure the reaction was quite different.

Winning over the hearts and minds of the business can seem tricky, but with a few techniques, it will be easier to get them to say, "You don't understand, our Compliance Officer is Awesome!"

Have a Whiskey and Stay Up Late

Yes, you heard me. Have a whiskey and stay up late. Although I am never the last person in the bar, I've surprised and delighted many a business person by being "normal" and enjoying a cocktail. Why is this such an important thing? It's not the alcohol per se. If you don't drink for religious or personal reasons, you shouldn't drink to fit in, but rather, you need to let your hair down in whatever way is comfortable for you, because it shows you are human. Humans need to relax. Humans aren't always "good" and aren't always "on." They misbehave, stay up later than they should, have one too many drinks, occasionally smoke a cigarette or cigar, and wear relaxed clothes after hours. When you're invited out to be one of the "gang," try to be as comfortable as possible and fit in. You will win so many points by showing that you're "just like us" (whoever "us" is) whenever you can.

Please let me be clear – this advice shouldn't violate your sense of propriety. You shouldn't ever ignore your own sense of personal ethics or religious morality. However, to the extent you are comfortable joining in with the crowd, join in! Where you don't morally object, or where the activity involved doesn't offend you religious sensibilities, be present, especially after hours.

I've known many colleagues in the compliance profession who choose to answer emails and "be responsible" during the hour or two after business meetings. Don't do it. Go to the cocktail hour, even if you're getting a soda water with lemon, so you are perceived as part of the club.

You will be infinitely more effective when the people around you feel like you are one of them, and that emphatically includes socializing. Make time to socialize and to be present during "down time."

I have read many books and articles that state that women in particular, don't understand the value of participating in post-meeting revelry. Women tend to be responsibility-oriented, and sometimes we don't understand the value of spending the hour after the all-day board meeting chatting over cocktails about upcoming holiday plans. The reality is, relationships are critical. The more of a whole person you become to your Power Sources, the more Wildly Effective you can be.

Connecting through Commonality

Do you have children? A cat, dog, or bunny? A passion for movies or TV? A hatred for the current weather? Ah – you've got something in common with your co-workers! Compliance officers, lawyers, and other very responsible people can underestimate the importance of sharing the details of their lives, and engaging in mundane conversation with people within the organization. I'm here to tell you, time spent discussing the weather, your weekend plans, or how good the tacos are in your business park is time well spent!

I can't tell you the number of times someone has said to me, "Wow, you're actually really nice. To tell you the truth, I didn't think you'd be nice, or that we'd have anything in common, but did you know I have a dog, too? I got him at the shelter, and his name is..." I've watched the same phenomenon with people with children talking about schools and school choices.

Your job is to become a trusted advisor and friend to the business. Your job is to advise the business, but also to be the ally and sounding board for the businessmen and businesswomen who lead your organization. When you talk about your kids, pets, the weather, your weekend, or any other day-to-day topic, you make yourself more human, and more relatable. Don't underestimate the power of the mundane water-cooler conversations. If you don't ever participate in the conversations about the latest movies, TV shows or holidays, you are robbing yourself of a major business advantage.

Your Office: The Power of Personal Photos

Consider your office. In the book "Nice Girls Don't Get the Corner Office," author Lois P. Frankel states that women should not decorate their offices in an overly feminine way (including pictures of kids, pets or travels), unless that person is in a position of power which invokes fear. According to the author, if your position invokes fear, pictures of pets, kids or travels can make you more accessible, and make people more likely both to relate to you and to talk to you about important issues after they have "broken the ice" with light conversation.[8]

Compliance Officers have a bad reputation for being rigid disciplinarians. Heck, before I was a Chief Compliance Officer I would get nervous if I got an unexpected call from the Compliance Department! In order to humanize yourself, put up at least one picture of your pets, kids, siblings, family, or a vacation photo, so you can easily talk about something other than work. I have a casual photo of myself with my husband in my office, as well as a world map. People who come to talk to me sometimes ask about my travels and where I'm going next. The map gives me an opportunity to talk about my work, but also to share some of the interesting stories that come out of my travels.

Your goal is to become a person – a "real" person – to the people in your company. This sounds like an easy task, but in my experience it may be the hardest thing you do as a compliance officer. Until people experience you as someone they can trust, you will not be a Wildly Effective compliance officer. At best, you will be someone they don't mind; at worst, you will be someone they actively avoid or try to get around. To be Wildly Effective, connect on a personal level, and don't let the personal connections fade. Your effectiveness depends on it.

Avoiding No When Possible

Another way to build a bridge to the business is by avoiding the word "no" whenever you can. Don't misunderstand; as a Compliance Officer I know we have to deliver unpopular news on a regular basis. If we don't say no, we end up risking being publically shamed, as the BNP Paribas compliance team was in 2014. Because of the genocide in Darfur, the United States and other countries had placed economic sanctions against Sudan. BNP Paribas was the long-standing bank for many sanctioned Sudanese entities and people, and it had much to lose if it complied with the sanctions. The compliance officer famously (or infamously) stated, "The relationship with this body of counterparties is a historical one and the commercial stakes are significant. For these reasons, Compliance does not want to stand in the way of maintaining this activity."[9]

Compliance's job is to get in the way of illegal and unethical activity. However, to become indispensable to the business, you must communicate your decisions in a way that treats the requestor with respect, and in a timeframe and manner that shows you legitimately considered whether it was possible to comply with the request in an ethical way. When you must say no, consider the following techniques.

Suggest an Alternative

If the business wants to work with a competitor to go into a new market, the obvious answer is no. However, perhaps there is a way in which the two companies can work together where they don't compete. Perhaps the people working on the new project could be consolidated into a new subsidiary in a different office space that is walled off from information that could be considered commercially sensitive, or that could lead to an accusation of competition violations.

Before saying no, try working with the businesspeople to find an alternative. Even if you are unable to find an alternative, you are much more likely to engender the goodwill of the business when you work with them to find an alternative, rather than just saying "no." Teaming with the business to find an alternative lets the Power Sources know you are pro-business, and you understand the importance of the product your company sells.

If you ultimately say no, you will do so with the business feeling that they can work with you, and that you will do your best for them and the company in the future or on other projects. The Power Sources will be much more likely to bring their next concern to you, rather than trying to work around you, if they are confident you will work to find a compliant alternative to any unacceptable proposition.

Explain Yourself

When I was a child, if I asked my father for something and he refused, my sisters and I would ask "Why!?!" repeatedly. After giving a reasonable answer, if asked again, he would shut down the discussion by saying, "Because I'm the father, that's why." Although this type of tongue-in-cheek answer may work with five-year olds, it doesn't go over well with adults who expect rational answers.

Some compliance officers are offended when they have to explain themselves or the law. I worked with an arrogant and difficult in-house counsel at one time, who felt his word was absolute. In fact, when challenged on a decision he'd made, he'd talk down to the business person, implying that the law was far too complicated to be explained, and he didn't have time to explain it anyway, because he was far too busy being important. This approach backfired, as business people learned to work around him whenever possible.

By contrast, one of the best strategies I've come across for becoming a Wildly Effective compliance officer is to explain why the business is or is not allowed to do whatever it is they wish to do.

Many compliance officers have attended law school, where professors direct the students to write using the "IRAC" formula. The "I" stands for issue, "R" stands for rule, "A" stands for analysis, and "C" stands for conclusion. I've found this writing formula to be particularly effective when crafting a response to a businessman or woman who has asked a question about an issue that involves the law.

For example, let's say that you work in the music business. The marketing team wants to give T-shirts and free tickets to the police force, whose members will be helping to protect the fans and the musicians at a concert in Paris. The response to the business could simply be "NO," or "No, that's against our gifts and hospitality policy." However, a much more compelling answer could be written using the IRAC format:

Dear Power Source,

(ISSUE) Thank you for your question regarding whether you can give free t-shirts and concert tickets to the police force that will be protecting our employees, the fans and the musicians at our upcoming concert in Paris. (RULE) Unfortunately, our company is governed by the anti-bribery laws of the United States and United Kingdom, and those laws impose big penalties for the bribery of government officials. (ANALYSIS) While I certainly believe that these presents are not meant to be bribes, the intent could be misconstrued. Secondarily, our Gifts and Hospitality Policy does not allow these types of presents to be given to government officials, and according to the definition of government official in our policy, the police are government officials. (CONCLUSION). For these reasons, we cannot give out the t-shirts or tickets to the police force. I apologize if this creates any problems for you.

This email is written concisely, so the person reading it will understand why you made your decision. It is much easier to win the hearts and minds of the employees and Power Sources when you explain to them why you made your decision. No one likes to feel that they are the victim of arbitrary rule-making. By explaining the law or policy behind your decision, you will be Wildly Effective because the business will know it can trust you to make reasoned decisions that will both protect the company and promote the products the company sells whenever possible.

Use the Band-Aid Approach

If you have to say no, do so in the same way you'd deal with a bandage: quickly and with as little pain as possible. I have worked in several environments where the approach of legal personnel or managers was to simply hold requests they did not want to answer for as long as possible, in the hopes that the request might become out of date or go away. I have never understood this approach. It leads to incredible frustration and to the breakdown of trust between the business and the person with the power to grant approval.

If you have to say no, do it quickly.

If you have to say no, do it quickly. By "quickly" I mean as soon as you have a definitive answer. The business will be much happier knowing they need to come up with a different approach than if they are left waiting while you appear to do nothing in response to their request.

Another tip for being Wildly Effective — keep the requesting party in the loop, and give estimates for when you will have an answer. You may not know exactly when you will be able to give a final answer to the business, but a short email like the following will go a long way towards building trust and creating the right expectations. Try something like, "Thank you for your question. I need to take this to outside counsel to review. I should have an answer for you in three weeks. If it is going to take longer than that, or if I need additional information, I will contact you."

Focus on what's Important to THEM, not YOU

Typically, the first thing you do as a compliance officer is to perform a risk assessment or review the one previously completed. You've got multiple priorities; for instance, the ethics helpline needs to be registered with the data protection authority in Europe, the Chinese sales team needs in-person antitrust training, and you need to update the Code of Conduct. How do you determine the order in which you tackle equally high-ranking issues? Easy — first do what the Power Sources will value the most, and then do the rest of the tasks.

Give Them what They Want First

Why should you start with the task the Power Sources will value most? To begin with, the Power Sources are much more likely to value you if they perceive you to be of value to THEM. When you give the Power Sources what they have been asking for, you are much more likely to be valued. You are also more likely to be able to leverage the Power Sources to obtain buy-in for your remaining high-impact tasks, as you have established good will with the Power Sources. Start with what the Power Sources want, and make sure you explicitly tell them about the accomplishment when it is finished.

Use Your Risk Assessment to Ask for what You Want

Once you've completed the important tasks required by the Power Sources, then go through the remainder of the tasks assigned to you with assistance from the Power Sources. If you've successfully tapped into the Power Sources' Primary Motivators, and you've given them what they want, you should have strong allies that will serve you well in difficult times.

Connecting to the Power Sources can be done in multiple ways. In later chapters, you'll learn advanced persuasion techniques to continue the Power Sources' interest in your work.

When in Rome...On Connecting in Foreign Places

One of my favorite things about working in compliance is the ability to travel as part of my duties. Since beginning my compliance career, I have trained employees, lawyers and business people on five continents in more than thirty-five countries. There is an art to winning the trust, respect and admiration of people who live outside your country. Let me share my best tips for doing so.

Get Your Teenage Euro-Trip Wonder and Appreciation Back

"WOW!" should be your favorite word when travelling abroad for work. If you are lucky enough to be able to travel outside of your home country, remember back to the first time you went abroad. Can you re-member the wonder you felt when you realized people didn't speak your language? Can you remember the fascination you had when you realized people ate foods you'd never heard of, or had animals for pets that you ate? Can you remember the salty sweet taste of your Italian cheese in Italy, or eating kangaroo in Australia? Can you remember your first fiery bite of Mexican food in Mexico, or the steam coming off your first dish of street noodles in Singapore? Travel expands who you are, and that is an amazing experience.

It is easy to become jaded when you travel for business. Sometimes it feels that all you ever see is the inside of the Hilton Hotel. But a certain amount of your experience when traveling for business is a choice. If you choose to get up early to go for a walk in the city center, or go out at night for an ice cream or beer outside the hotel bar, you will have a vastly richer experience. You must choose to make time in your travels to explore.

Once you do, you will greatly enhance your experience of the business, and the cultures in which the business operates. Understanding the culture will make you Wildly Effective, as you can talk to people in far-flung places from first-hand experience.

I have been lucky enough to have travelled nearly every month for the past several years. Has it always been easy or fun? Absolutely not. I am not immune to rage when my flight has been delayed for the sixth time and I'm not going to be home for an important event. I have also visited places I never thought I'd want to go. However, I've learned that there is always a choice. You can choose to return to the wonder and excitement of the unusual and distinct, or you can be blasé. I promise you, choosing excitement is always a better choice! Not only do you have a better time, you are much more likely to engage the people who live in the foreign land.

Do Your Research

When you find out you're going to a new place, the first thing you should do is start researching. When I found out that I was going to do training in Albania, my original thought was, "Where is Albania?" (Answer: near Greece and Macedonia). A month later I learned that I would be going to Jakarta. I knew little of Indonesia other than that Bali was supposed to have great beaches, and I enjoyed the sections of "Eat, Pray, Love" that took place there. I didn't know anything about Indonesia's capital city of Jakarta or Albania's capital city of Tirana. I didn't know about either places' religion, history, weather, landscape or people. But I was eager to learn!

Whenever I know I am going to visit a country to do training or an internal investigation, I begin with learning. At a minimum, I work through the following checklist:

- What is the basic history of the country? With which countries have they had wars?

- What are the majority and minority religions in the country? How tolerant is the general public about other religions? Does the government or state enforce religion?
- Are women's rights, gay/lesbian rights, and other rights endorsed or rejected?
- What language is spoken?
- Is there a history of colonization in the country? If so, which country was the colonizing country?
- What is the major industry of the country?
- How does the country's population generally feel about alcohol, smoking, Americans, English-speakers, and eating beef, pork, shrimp, seafood or animals in general?

By completing some basic research, you will find yourself much more likely to ask informed questions, and much less likely to make major cultural mistakes. Research about the history of a people is likely to pay big dividends, because nearly everyone is extremely proud of his or her culture. Showing interest in the culture and doing research beforehand shows a commitment to understanding. You don't come in as "the compliance officer here for two days." Instead, you come in as "Bob, who was so excited to try our food!" And speaking of food…

Let's Go To Your Favorite…

When I had been a Chief Compliance Officer for a grand total of five weeks, I headed out to my first tour of Southeast Asia, which included Malaysia, Singapore and Indonesia. When I arrived in Jakarta, Indonesia, I was surprised when the managers of the office took me for lunch to an upscale Italian restaurant. First of all, pizza in Indonesia leaves something to be desired compared to pizza in Italy, or even England. But more than that, I was eager to try Indonesian food. Why had they taken me to a pizza place? "We didn't think you'd want to try Indonesian food, so we took you here instead."

When in Rome, do as the Romans do. When in Jakarta, do as the Indonesians do, and eat beef rendang. No, seriously – do it! It's delicious! The lovely people at my company's Indonesian licensee wanted to make sure I was comfortable, and therefore they took me to the Italian place where they knew I would be comfortable. However, I won many more friends with my next question: "So, for dinner or lunch tomorrow, would you take me to your favorite local place to eat?" Memorize this question. Use it every time you travel. You will make loyal friends.

> *"So, for dinner or lunch tomorrow, would you take me to your favorite local place to eat?" Memorize this question. Use it every time you travel.*

I certainly don't like all foods. However, people have always taken me to fascinating places where I could try things I never would have eaten otherwise. That isn't always a good thing. I was once served cow brain in a curry sauce, but I tried one bite and then went on to the chili-flavored fried chicken. People were impressed with my "bravery," but more importantly, with my interest in their culture. The desire to try new things and to embrace their local favorites brings more good will than you can imagine. That good will tends to be reciprocal. If you're interested in them, they are likely to be more interested in you and what you have to say and teach.

Putting It Together

All of the previously mentioned techniques will help you to build the all-important emotional bridge to the business. The business is run by people who need to work with — or work around — the Compliance Department. By becoming more human to the men and women who work in your business, you'll be more likely to be seen as a trusted ally.

Now, let's talk about some specialized techniques regarding talking and listening that will help you to be Wildly Effective.

Chapter 6: Hear and Be Heard!

To be a Wildly Effective compliance officer, you must master two related skills — you must HEAR and BE HEARD. Being heard is critical, because you cannot be effective unless the employees and management hear what you are saying and act on what they hear. But just as importantly, you must learn to really hear what is going on around you. If you have not integrated yourself as a trusted asset to the business, you will not have the opportunity to hear what is really going on. In this chapter, you'll learn secret skills to get to the heart of what the business is saying. You'll also learn surprising ways to be heard, so your message gets across loud and clear. Perhaps most critically, you'll learn the ways you might unintentionally block communication. Once you avoid these, you are much more likely to be Wildly Effective!

Salesmanship and Listening

When you think of great salesmanship (or saleswomanship), you probably imagine a fast-talking huckster out to convince you to part with your cash before he gets run out of town on a rail. Not surprisingly, there is a better way to sell than to swindle people. There are many masters of sales methodology. One of these masters is David Sandler, the creator of the Sandler System. According to David Sandler, the key to great sales-manship is listening.

The Sandler System is built on one fundamental idea: when a sales person is dealing with a prospect, s/he should be listening 70% of the time and talking only 30% of the time. So how does listening create sales?

> *The Sandler System is built on one fundamental idea: when a sales person is dealing with a prospect, s/he should be listening 70% of the time and talking only 30% of the time.*

Listening creates goodwill between the person talking and the person listening. It also enables you to get to the heart of the problem, which will allow you to offer a truly helpful solution.

But what's Really Bothering Me...

Have you ever had a phone call with your mother or a good friend that went something like this, "Hi there! How am I? Oh, things aren't great, to be honest. I just bought paint to do up the hallway and it is too bright a shade of white. Hmmm, my sister just cancelled lunch with me for tomorrow. What else? Oh – Dave came home last night after midnight. Can you imagine? How many times do I have to ask him to come home in time to say goodnight to the kids. I'm starting to think something bad is going on..."

If you weren't practicing the Sandler method, you might have immediately offered to bring over your leftover paint in Touch of Cream, with satin finish. The conversation would probably have gone off into decorating. Instead, by allowing your friend to talk, you allowed her *to find out what was really bothering her.* When people are allowed to talk, it often becomes like an onion. You start out with the hard outer layer, but as the person keeps talking, the inner layers of critical information appear. Often people don't consciously know what is bothering them the most. When you allow them to talk, you give them the gift of *discovering what is really wrong.*

So how does this apply to compliance? When an employee comes to see you, let them talk 70% of the time. Use open-ended questions that allow them to really say what they think. Try questions and statements like:

- Oh, that's interesting. Tell me about that.
- Is there anything else you'd like to tell me?
- Is there anything else that I should know?

When you invite people to talk, you invite them to tell you everything.

Whistle-blowing and Letting Them Talk

Safecall is a terrific company I've used for whistle-blower hotline services. They do things differently than other providers I've seen. Safecall exclusively employs former policemen and policewomen as their report takers. Safecall also takes every call, despite the possibility that certain data protection laws may limit the acceptable types of calls to financially-related topics. For example, in many Nordic countries, employees may only call the whistle-blower hotline to report incidents related to fraud, bribery and other proscribed topics.

Why would Safecall allow reports on all kinds of topics to be taken? Because in their extensive experience, very few people really know why they are calling, and if you let them talk, they'll start to volunteer really important information. Think about the following two scenarios.

In scenario one, employee Juan is upset with his boss, who has been sexually harassing Juan's friend Shelby. If Juan calls a traditional whistle-blower hotline operated by his company's vendor, Juan will first be asked if his report is about fraud or a financial crime. Juan will say no and be turned away.

However, in scenario two, if Juan calls a company like Safecall, he may start the conversation saying, "Hi, my boss is sexually harassing my friend Shelby." He will be asked for specifics, and then asked, "Is there anything else you can tell me about this situation?" Suddenly Juan remembers that his boss has been submitting inaccurate expense reports, and having shrouded conversations with the director of a competing company. By letting Juan talk, the company is much more likely to get all of the information they need to respond to the complaint.

As a compliance officer, you always want to get to the root of the problem. Many people don't have the background to know that the complaint they are making may trigger a trade sanctions issue. They may not know that the uncomfortable conversation they heard at an industry awards show could be a violation of competition law, or constitute collusion. They almost certainly won't know that in many countries, the company could collect evidence, talk to the regulator, and get immunity for disclosing a competition violation before any other company offers evidence. Allowing people to talk has the advantage of giving you the best chance to do your job in a Wildly Effective way.

Listening Creates an Investment in YOU

Another reason that the Sandler Method of allowing people to talk 70% of the time is so effective is because many social scientists believe the deepest longing of the human heart is to be known and heard by another. When you really focus on someone and listen to what they have to say, the speaker becomes invested in you. When you sense it is time to offer a solution, the speaker will really feel that he or she has been listened to. Social mores create a situation where, after someone has listened to one person, the other is obligated to return the favor. By carefully listening to the complainer, you will have created a desire in that person to listen to you in return.

If you spend your time in conversation thinking about what you'll say next, rather than focusing on what the speaker is saying, you deprive the speaker of the gift of your full attention. You also deprive yourself of the opportunity to be Wildly Effective, because the speaker isn't given the opportunity to fully invest in you.

Showing the Walk and Walking the Talk

Here are some top ways to show people you are listening. The first one is to mirror their language. Mirroring someone's language means taking what they say and reflecting those exact same words back to them. One of my colleagues observed this at a call center for his company. He was trying to figure out how to make the employees more effective when dealing with complaints. An irate customer called one of the agents, and he listened in:

> Customer: I've been on hold for twenty minutes! I can't tell you how angry I am!

> Employee: I'm so sorry that you feel inconvenienced.

> Customer: I don't feel inconvenienced. I am angry!

> Employee: Sir, I apologize for the irritation.

> Customer: You guys have made me so angry!

> Employee: Yes, I understand that you're frustrated.

> Customer: I'm NOT FRUSTRATED! YOU'RE MAKING ME ANGRY!

How much better would it have been for the customer if the employee had changed his tactic and mirrored the exact language used by the customer.

> Customer: I've been on hold for twenty minutes! I can't tell you how angry I am!

> Employee: I understand that you're angry, sir. How can I help you today?

Using someone's exact language makes them feel heard. Once an angry or defensive person feels heard, a subtle shift usually occurs, making him or her more able to listen.

Using Their Lingo

In the book "How to Make Anyone Fall in Love with You," author Leil Lowndes used social science research to prove that an important way to make someone feel like you understand their world is to use their words to describe their job.[10] For instance, a lawyer or architect works "at the firm," while a musician "goes to a gig." Some people "graft," others simply work.

When you meet with an employee, pay attention to the words he or she uses regarding work. Mirror the language that they use. Does the person describe their assigned helper as a "secretary," "personal assistant," "p.a.," "executive assistant," "admin," or something else? Mirror their language choice to show that you understand them. They will respond with more detail because you have shown that you understand their world.

Using the Summary Technique

Here's a great strategy to ensure the person with whom you're speaking feels heard — let the person talk until the conversation hits a natural stopping point, summarize what has been said, then ask if you got it right. Here's an example:

Manager Mike: I'm so frustrated with my sub-contractor on the job in Lille! Roger keeps failing to give me receipts for any of his purchases. He has hired two consultants, but hasn't given me the reason for hiring them, so I can't finish my paperwork, and now he's resisting the audit. Ugh!

Compliance Kristy: Ugh, that sounds frustrating. So Roger isn't giving you receipts, won't give you paperwork related to the consultants, and is resisting the audit. Have I got that right?

From here, Mike is likely to expand on each of his frustrations. The other possibility is that Mike will give you more information, or go in a new direction, showing you other potential problems. Lastly, Mike may tell you (1) yes, you've got it right or (2) no, you didn't understand correctly. Either of these options is fantastic, because if you've got it right, then you can immediately work on finding a solution to Mike's problem. If you didn't understand correctly, then you are able to ask further questions to ensure you have it right, so you can come up with a great solution.

But Don't Do This!

David Sandler's method focuses on listening and clear communication to seal the deal. Imagine the following common scenario:

Manager Mike: Hi, Compliance Kristy. I'm having a problem. I'm worried because we used a consultant in Latin America for a project recently, and I can't understand why we needed to hire her, or what she did for the company.

Compliance Kristy: Oh, no! Well you should rest assured, Mike, that our ABC program is top notch. But to clear this up for you, I'll ask the consultant to complete the DDQ, and we'll put her in the GRC system. We'll also run a Bridger check to make sure she's not on the OFAC SDN list, just in case. Don't you worry, it'll all be A-OK.

Manager Mike: Uh huh.

It is so easy to get caught up in compliance speak. Sandler is adamant that sales are lost due to people using acronyms that aren't understood by the other person. Why does this ruin the sale?

- The person listening to you feels dumb. The listener feels he or she should understand, but doesn't.
- The person listening to you feels out of the loop.

- The person listening to you feels irritated that you think you're better or smarter than he or she.

What will the person do in response? Usually one of two things: (1) pretend to understand, and then leave the conversation as quickly as possible or (2) tune you out, determining that whatever you said doesn't apply to him or her.

You cannot connect to someone when you use language they do not understand. To be a Wildly Effective compliance officer, you must put yourself in the shoes of the other person and ensure they understand what you are saying. You are not only responsible for what you say. You are responsible for what they understand.

> *You are not only responsible for what you say. You are responsible for what they understand.*

Social scientists have proven people are more motivated to move away from fear and discomfort than to move toward a something they want.[11] By using compliance-speak, YOU become their source of discomfort, so they will want to move away from you. This is not what you want! By listening effectively, mirroring the language of the person who is talking, and then responding with a positive and proactive answer, you will be Wildly Effective in responding to problems and gathering facts.

Know When to Stop Talking

Sandler's system teaches salespeople to STOP talking once they've got the sale. He gives examples of people talking themselves out of a sale by continuing to give unnecessary details that confuse the prospect until the prospect decides he should think it over some more.

How does this apply to a compliance officer? Imagine you're going before the Board to request a new Governance Risk and Compliance tracking system that will allow your team around the world to view the status of cases. The new system will cost $20,000 more than is currently in the budget. You've talked about a recent disaster that could have been averted, and given a demonstration of the system to the Board. The Chairwoman of the Board says, "Yes, I can see why that would be helpful. Let's do it." Then the compliance officer says, "That's great! And let me show you the four other features that the system has. The first one…"

STOP! STOP while you are ahead. Once you've gotten what you want, STOP talking. People talk themselves out of sales, dates, jobs, and getting what they want all the time by not knowing when to be quiet. If you've received a yes to your request, stop talking. Say thank you very much, and leave. Or if it is inappropriate to leave, turn the conversation to another topic. Whatever you do, stop talking about your win and move on.

Now that you know the basics of listening and being heard, it's time to move on to really provocative persuasion techniques which will catapult you into the stratosphere to make you Wildly Effective.

Chapter 7: Super-Secret Advanced Persuasion Techniques

You're now at the part of the book where the groundwork has been laid for the really advanced techniques. You've mastered the Four Motivators, and are certain you have specific stories in your training and presentations that relate to all of them. You've identified the Primary Motivator of your most important Power Sources. You're ready to go from being great at your job to being Wildly Effective, using the additional techniques you're about to learn.

Is it Ethical to Use These Techniques?

The first time I gave a seminar during a conference discussing the advanced techniques you'll read about below, one of the members of the audience was furious. Her eyes shot daggers at me, and during the question and answer session following the talk, she stood up and said, "We've been hearing all about ethics and motivating people to do the right thing. But now you're telling us how to manipulate people using fear. Is that ethical?"

To answer her question, I drew on insights from the book "Yes! 50 Scientifically Proven Ways to be Persuasive." In this book, author Robert Cialdini notes that being persuasive and using human psychology in a powerful way is ethically neutral.[12] In other words, it isn't inherently good or bad to be influential and persuasive. These techniques can be used in ethical or unethical ways. Is it more ethical to use these techniques to create a more law-abiding society and a happier employee base, or to fail by not using the techniques that will make you a Wildly Effective compliance officer? I assume since you're reading this book that you are interested in making a difference in ethics and compliance. The advanced techniques you'll read about below will take you from good to outstanding.

Use Fear, but Follow Up with Specific Actions

In the 1960s, Yale researcher Howard Leventhal performed an experiment about the use of fear, and how people respond to being frightened. Leventhal told his volunteer students they were to review a pamphlet about the dangers of tetanus, and the importance of obtaining a tetanus shot to avoid the disease. One group was given a "high fear" brochure which included scary stories about the ravages of the disease. The other group was given a "low fear" brochure, which described the disease and the injection that would inoculate against it. Leventhal thought his experiment would prove that the high-fear brochure was more effective in creating action than the low-fear brochure. However, that didn't happen. When the students left the room, only one of them from either group sought out a tetanus shot from the campus health-care center. When Leventhal's researchers followed up with the students, he found that each had understood the risk of the disease, and understood the shot would inoculate them against it. But they still hadn't gone to get the shot.

Leventhal then performed a second version of the experiment. This time, he gave some students a pamphlet on tetanus by itself. Other students were given a pamphlet with a map and instructions to the on-campus health center where the students could obtain the shot. Thirty-three percent of the group given the map and instructions went to get the shot, a ten-fold uptick from the previous experiment.

Leventhal concluded that fear by itself paralyses people. However, fear induced, then followed by specific, actionable steps, strongly persuades people into action.[13] The students who were given the brochure without the instructions found themselves paralyzed by fear, but without any way to alleviate the discomfort.

> *"The more clearly people see behavioral means for ridding themselves of fear, the less they will need to resort to denial." – Robert Ciadini* [14]

How do we use these observations in compliance? When you use fear, you must do so in conjunction with specific, actionable steps, or you risk your audience being paralyzed. Let's see this in action:

Compliance Kate: So you see, Mr. Chairman, the whistle-blower complaint about the illegal payments made in our Nigerian headquarters is almost certainly true. We have to decide now whether we should self-disclose to the Department of Justice.

Mr. Chairman: Good grief! What could happen?!?

Compliance Kate: Well, our competitor Ziplan had a $100 million fine imposed, and faced debarment over a similar incident last year.

Mr. Chairman: Well, that couldn't happen to us. You must be mistaken. Look, I'm friends with Elian, who runs that company. He's a great guy. Go back and try to find some more information. Your initial conclusion can't be right, and I won't see Elian's name run through the mud.

When the compliance officer delivers bad news, the person hearing it will immediately be in discomfort. People move away from fear and discomfort, and the compliance officer is in the position of creating these unwanted emotions. If the fear is created, but not followed up by a specific, actionable measure, the person listening will decide one of two things: (1) The risk isn't as big as it sounds, so I won't do anything about it (paralysis), or (2) this doesn't apply to me, I don't need to worry about it (denial). Either of these reactions will not serve to make you Wildly Effective.

Let's see what happens when the compliance officer offers specific, actionable measures:

Compliance Kate: So you see, Mr. Chairman, the whistle-blower complaint about the illegal payments made in our Nigerian headquarters is almost certainly true. We may have to decide if we should self-disclose to the Department of Justice. I've already contacted the law firm of Blinking and Grede to begin the analysis. They did a great job with a similar investigation in South Africa last year, so I have the utmost faith in their capacities. We've also put the person who was accused of making the payment on leave until we can sort out what happened, and I'm going to Nigeria next week to do follow-up anti-bribery training with our staff.

Mr. Chairman: OK. This is terrible news, but it sounds like you've got it handled for the moment. What could happen?

Compliance Kate: Well, our competitor Ziplan had a $100 million fine imposed, and faced debarment over a similar incident last year. But they didn't self-disclose, and they covered up the whistle-blower complaint. We've taken proactive steps to be sure that doesn't happen here.

Mr. Chairman: Thanks. I want a full update on this as soon as possible.

In the second example, Compliance Kate used fear successfully to communicate the gravity of the situation, but she also provided immediate, specific actionable measures. In this way, instead of being *the creator of discomfort*, she becomes *the creator of the solution to the fear*, meaning the listener will want to get closer to her, and to listen to what she has to say.

Fear, when properly used, can create tremendous impetus for change. Fear for Self and Fear for the Business are powerful Primary Motivators. Many top executives and board members will be strongly motivated by fear, but in order for you to exploit the fear positively to get the resources you need for your program, you must harness that fear with specific, actionable measures.

Never go into a board meeting or discussion with your managers with bad news or concerns without proposing specific, actionable measures. If you do, you will end up in a worse position than when you started. Instead, bring ideas with you. Even if the board or managers hate your ideas, you have something to work with to create a solution that is comfortable for the people involved.

Fear is potent stuff. Use it to your advantage by saving the day with your specific, actionable measures. It'll make you the hero, which makes the listener much less likely to shoot the messenger.

> *Never go into a board meeting or discussion with your managers with bad news or concerns without proposing specific, actionable measures. If you do, you will end up in a worse position than when you started. Instead, bring ideas about solutions with you.*

People Buy with Emotion, then Justify with Logic

Has your co-worker ever told you that they were going to buy a Toyota, but then came into the office talking about their new Mercedes? What does that fact tell you about the choice? The conversation usually goes something like this: "Well, the Toyota was great, but the Mercedes gets 4 miles to the gallon more than the Toyota. Also, the Mercedes has a far superior safety record, and it is only $150 more per month on the special lease option I got. Plus, my wife has always wanted a Mercedes, and the Toyota wasn't available in Midnight Blue. The Mercedes was everything I wanted." Is this person speaking from logic or emotion?

A major tenet of the Sandler Method is that *people buy with emotion, then justify with logic.*[15] Was the Mercedes objectively a better choice for your co-worker? Probably not, but the emotional desire to have the Mercedes overrode the desire for the Toyota. Your co-worker's brain followed emotion, then came up with logical reasons why the Mercedes was the better choice.

For the compliance officer, this is powerful information. A Wildly Effective compliance officer will use emotion to get buy-in from the decision-maker, and then use logic to justify the decision-maker's choice. Which emotion should be used? When you discover which of the Four Primary Motivators resonates most with your decision-maker, you can use that Motivator to connect to that person's emotions.

For example, let's say you need to buy sanctions screening software in order to ensure you aren't working with anyone on the Office of Foreign Asset Control's Specially Designated National List. Having followed the method outlined in earlier chapters, you learned that your CEO's Primary Motivator is Fear for Self. You should hook into the emotion of this CEO by telling her about a situation where another CEO was fined, publically shamed, or lost her job for sanctions violations. Then, explain how the sanctions screening software will protect the company and her. Once the CEO has identified with the Fear for Self, your logical solution will be very appealing. The CEO will be able to justify the need for a larger budget, the tools you need, more staff, etc., much more easily, simply because the logic supports the emotion.

Let's try another example. If your company's sales manager is motivated primarily by Competitive Edge, your job is first to appeal to her competitive nature by telling her about how much the new product or promotion can increase sales or visibility for the company. Once you've connected to that Competitive Edge emotion, you can give the logistical information (including price, resource request, etc.) which will then be used to justify the decision to buy the product.

People can do an amazing job of justifying their purchases once they've decided to make them. The often repeated maxim, "People love to buy but hate to be sold" comes from the experience of being around a salesperson who is selling with logic before the person's emotions are sold. Once a person has emotionally bought in, the details are simply the details.

Would You Please Do Me a Favor?

Benjamin Franklin performed a social experiment way back when he was in the Pennsylvania legislature. Mr. Franklin was bothered by the staunch political opposition of another member of the governing body. He decided to try to win the affection of his then-enemy by asking him for a favor. Mr. Franklin asked his opponent if he could borrow a rare book that he knew was in the man's collection. Mr. Franklin described what happened as follows:

> I wrote a note to him, expressing my desire of perusing that book, and requesting he would do me the favor of lending it to me for a few days. He sent it immediately, and I return'd it in about a week with another note, expressing strongly my sense of the favor. When we next met in the House, he spoke to me (which he had never done before), and with great civility; and he ever manifested a readiness to serve me on all occasions, so that we became great friends, and our friendship continued to his death. This is another instance of the truth of an old maxim I had learned, which says, "He that has once done you a kindness will be more ready to do you another, than he whom you yourself have obliged."[16]

Social scientists report that this anecdote and additional studies have proven that when a person does a favor for you, their respect for you increases.[17] In fact, even if the person previously did not like you, they are more likely to believe themselves to be fond of you after doing a favor for you. Why? Because people do not like to behave inconsistently with their beliefs. Therefore, *if they have performed a favor for you, or gone out of their way to help you, they* **must** *like you.* Why else would they behave that way?

Knowing this, it is imperative you ask those whom you wish to influence to do a favor to help you. Ask the CEO to write an open letter supporting Compliance and Ethics Week that you can post on your intranet. Ask a member of the Board to introduce you to one of his or her acquaintances. Ask the accounting manager to speak about the newest policy at a meeting you are facilitating. By asking for a favor, you are actually increasing the likelihood that the decision-maker will support you in the future.

What Kind of Favor?

Ask for a small favor to begin with. Social science has proven that people are more likely to say yes to subsequent requests, once they've said yes the first time.[18] As an example, studies have proven that once a person has given any amount to a charity, they are much more likely to give money to that charity when solicited a second or third time. This is why many charities have adopted a motto saying that "even a penny helps," or "whatever you have to give, it will make a difference." Although it is certainly true that when aggregated, small amounts of change can create large amounts of money, the reason many charities have adopted this tactic is because subsequent requests for donations have a much higher likelihood of success if the person has already donated.[19]

I have seen this work in my own life. I travel frequently for my job and for leisure. As I live in England, I usually fly British Airways. British Airways has a charity called "Flying Start," where they collect money in any currency and any amount to support children around the world. They provide little envelopes in which travelers can leave their change. The first time I donated, I gave my coins from a trip I'd taken to the United States. I felt good knowing I'd helped. From that trip on, I've often brought extra coins with me so I can put them in the envelope and hand them to the steward or stewardess on my way out of each flight.

Why do I look forward to giving away my coins on flights? Social scientists believe this once again proves people like to live up to their beliefs about themselves. Once I had given my change to Flying Start, I identified myself as someone who supported children through the Flying Start charity. After I had self-identified in that way, I was much more likely to continue to act in accordance with that belief.

How do you put this knowledge to work? In your job, when you go to ask the CEO to write the post for the intranet in support of Compliance and Ethics Week, offer to write it so that it doesn't take any time out of the CEO's schedule. Ask the Sales Manager to introduce the new policy at your meeting but offer to write the introduction for him, and then stand up after the introduction and explain the policy yourself. Little favors create a strong impetus to say yes to larger favors. See the little favor as the opportunity to get your foot in the door. Once a person identifies herself as someone who (1) likes you and (2) supports you with her actions, you are well on your way to being a Wildly Effective compliance officer.

Once You Have Received a Favor or Two...

Once you've received a favor or two, ask for something really big. Ask for something that you want, but is far outside of what you expect to get. Then ask for something that would have been a stretch, but now seems much more reasonable. The sequence goes like this:

- Month One: Ask the CEO to write an email to post to the intranet supporting the new Gifts and Hospitality policy. Offer to write the post for her/him if it helps.
- Month Two: Ask the CEO to introduce you to the sales team at the annual meeting, and then give you ten minutes to say a few words.
- Month Three: Ask the CEO for a new Governance, Risk and Control system which costs a similar amount to your whole annual budget. The likelihood is that you'll be turned down.
- Soon thereafter, or at the same meeting: Ask for a 10% increase in your budget to supply higher-quality online training with a new vendor, offering short, vignette-sized videos that would resonate well with the staff.

Why is this effective? Because people don't like to say no, and when they do say no, they don't like to do it over and over again. Think about your experience as a teenager, or with your teenagers. What do teenagers excel at? Continually asking and pushing until they get what they want by repetitively making the case that they should get it. Parents get worn down, and tired of saying no. It is easier to give in to the smaller request than repeatedly say no to everything.

By asking for something you really want and need after asking for something you are unlikely to receive, you're in a much stronger psychological position with the decision-maker than you would be otherwise. This technique is most effective when used after you've already begun asking for and receiving favors.

This Word Will Make You More than 50 Percent More Persuasive

A research study was performed at the City University of New York some years ago. The experiment was conducted at one of the libraries on campus, where coin-operated photocopiers were in use. The experimenter approached 120 people just before they deposited their coins to start copying. The experimenter requested to use the copier before the person who was already at the machine.

When the experimenter used the phrase, "Excuse me, I have five pages, may I use the Xerox machine?" 60% of people complied with the request and allowed the experimenter to go ahead of him or her.

When the experimenter used the phrase, "Excuse me, I have five pages, may I use the Xerox machine because I have to make copies?" 93% of people complied with the request and allowed the experimenter to go ahead of him or her.[20]

What accounts for the tremendous increase in persuasion? The authors of the study concluded it was the use of the word "because."[21] People are much more likely to respond positively to a request if they know why you are asking. The experiment described above seems absurd — in both scenarios, the person is asking to go first because they want to make copies. However, when the reason was presented to the person at the copier, he or she was much more likely to comply.

How do you use this technique? Always give the reason for your request, and phrase the reason starting with the word because. To up the ante on this technique to its highest level, use the word "because" followed by an example from the person's Primary Motivator.

> *To up the ante on this technique to its highest level, use the word "because" followed by an example from the person's Primary Motivator.*

Let's say that Compliance Chris wants Manager Martin to push his sales team to put all agents through the new due diligence process. Manager Martin is motivated by Fear for the Business. He doesn't want to take the time to fill in the online information, and doesn't want to take the chance this new procedure will lower his team's productivity. Compliance Chris can make his case compelling by using the combination of because AND Martin's Primary Motivator.

> Martin, I understand your concerns, but this process is beneficial to you and your team because you won't be working with third-parties that could land us in litigation or an investigation. It will ensure that we won't lose business because our reputation could be damaged if we have an issue like our competitor. Remember when that issue happened at Salt Co.? The papers ran with it for months.

The combination of "because," followed by the Primary Motivator, creates a double-whammy of persuasion, making your objective much more likely to be met.

Tell Them Who They Are

People have a funny way of living up to the expectations we place on them. Marriage counselors tell spouses to look for the good in their spouse, and to tell the spouse they are loved and appreciated. If you're constantly accusing your spouse of cheating, it is much more likely that your spouse will eventually cheat on you, even if he or she wasn't inclined to do so in the beginning. More often than not, people behave as you expect them to behave.

How can you use this knowledge to become a Wildly Effective compliance officer? Tell people who you think they are. When someone is arguing with you, or doesn't understand why the compliance department requires him or her to jump through so many hoops, use phrases like the following:

> Alexander, I know that you're a good and ethical guy, so I'm sure it will be clear to you why we can't walk that close to the line. A person like you will know that we need to follow the rules.

> Susan, you are an ethics champion. I know this program may seem cumbersome, but someone like you can lead your team in understanding the long-term value that comes from doing the right thing.

Why does telling someone who they are produce the result you've planted in their mind? Because nearly everyone believes themselves to be a good and ethical person, and people like to live up to their own image of themselves. When you tell them *the specific way in which they are expected to be a good and ethical person*, and then they act in a way that is contrary to your statement, they have to override their own image of themselves. In telling someone who they are, you've aligned your image of them with their image of themselves, and told them how you expect them to behave in order to qualify as a good and ethical person.

Read the newspaper and you'll find that most people, including bank robbers and other criminals, believe themselves to be good people and to have good motives. Using people's natural tendencies to benefit your compliance agenda is a positive way to get people to behave in an ethical way.

Will this technique work with everyone? No, of course not. If someone is a fraudster, or is actively trying to thwart the law, then telling them that they are ethical is unlikely to change their behavior. However, since the vast majority of people believe themselves to be good and ethical people, your verbal affirmation of this assumption is likely to make their behavior match your expectations.

Using all of these techniques together is likely to make you infinitely more persuasive than you would be otherwise. When practiced consistently, these techniques can move you from being good at your job to being a Wildly Effective compliance officer.

CHAPTER **8**

Chapter 8: I'm the Expert

Ȳou are the CEO, and you are hiring a new compliance officer to handle your most profitable region. Who would you rather have working for you, Antonio or Barbara?

Antonio has a good background. He has already served the company for five years in Internal Audit. He wants to move into Compliance, and has good relationships with the business. Barbara is a noted Compliance expert who has published two articles on internal investigations in a trade magazine, and has recently been a speaker in a panel discussion on the future of compliance regulation in your industry. This is not a difficult choice, is it? Barbara, the Compliance Expert, will get the nod every time.

Managers and business people love experts. Your credibility, and your ability to get things done, will be greatly enhanced if the businesspeople you work with view you as an expert in your field. So, how do you become recognized as an expert in your field? It's easier than you might think.

While it is true that the techniques I will enumerate in this chapter definitely take time and energy, the dividends of that investment will follow you throughout your career. Becoming an expert in your field will set you up for future jobs, or for the possibility of consulting. Experts will always be in demand, and there is no better job security than being recognized as the go-to girl or guy in your industry.

Put It in Writing

The most effective way to establish yourself as an expert is to write about your topic. The gold standard is a published book, but obviously it is a rare compliance officer indeed who has the time, knowledge or inclination to write a book. Instead, many compliance officers write short articles or blogs that put their name out into the community. If you publish an article in a magazine, newspaper or other physical medium, it can be a brilliant calling card when you are applying for another job.

I've been publishing articles since I began my work in private practice. In 2011, I worked with cross-border discovery, electronic document review and production, in both Switzerland and the United Kingdom. While reviewing the current literature, I realized there was a great deal of confusion among practitioners about the complex rules affecting data transfer. Around this time, a group of experts in the U.S. calling themselves the Sedona Conference proposed a series of principles for electronic discovery. I thought Europeans might be interested in the principles put forward by the Sedona Conference, so I wrote a three-page article on the topic, which I submitted to Legal Week Magazine via Gibson Dunn's publicity department. Within a month, the story was accepted for publication, and I went from associate attorney to "published author."

After I wrote my first article, I wanted to write more. But I was afraid. I felt like a fraud. I was a young attorney. Who was I to write about data transfer from Europe and the U.K. to the U.S.? Did I really know anything useful enough to write about?

I had (and to a degree, still have) a classic case of Imposter Syndrome. Imposter Syndrome is the feeling that you're five minutes away from everyone discovering you don't know what you're doing and you don't know what you're talking about. Sheryl Sandberg discusses her Imposter Syndrome in her book "Lean In." She notes that it disproportionately affects women, but that men can have it as well.[22]

Even if you have doubts, you should still write. The process of writing and checking your facts will make you much more of an expert about your topic than you will ever be if you don't take the leap and start to write.

But how do you begin to write an article or to become an expert? The process of writing and publishing is easier when it is broken down into several steps.

Steps to Writing Your First Article

Step 1: Pick a topic you find interesting. This is important, as people will associate you with the topic going forward, and the topic will be associated with you when people Google your name. Do you want to be known as the go-to girl on supply chain audit for human rights? Do you want to write about retail antitrust topics for the foreseeable future? Think now about where this topic may lead.

Another approach suggested by author Joe Murphy is to find a topic you want or need to learn about, then start researching it. As you read good articles on the topic, reach out via email or phone to the authors of those works. As you get deeper into the topic it is very likely you will find unanswered questions or gaps that you can then fill with your work.

Step 2: Find a Hook. Find an angle to make people want to read the article. Writing about a new law is always popular, as is writing about an important court decision. You can also write about lessons learned from a recent prosecution or settlement.

Another way to find a hook is to look for an issue that people find confusing. For instance, I wrote an article in Compliance and Ethics Professional Magazine regarding the difference between "sensitive" personal data under European law, and what Americans think of as "sensitive" personal data. I chose to write about this topic because I've been in numerous conversations where Americans and Europeans have misunderstood each other about this issue.

Lastly, you can always write about your experience. Case studies are perennially popular, as practitioners want to know how YOUR company responded to an issue. One caveat — be careful when writing about your company's experience, as you will need the company's explicit permission before publishing such an article.

Step 3: Put yourself in the reader's shoes. Think about the target audience for your article, book, or blog post. What does this reader need to learn? Why is your article interesting? How will your reader be able to implement the changes you're suggesting? Make your article responsive to the needs of your community, and be sure that you speak directly to your audience. An academic article will have a very different length, structure and style than a blog post for a popular compliance-oriented website.

Step 4: Make your text sing. Use a catchy title to intrigue your audience. "How To" guides are always popular, as are numerical titles (e.g., "Five Ways to Dramatically Improve Training," or "Ten Ways to Engage the Board"). Contrarian titles are frequently popular as well (e.g., "Why the SEC's Enforcement Strategy is All Wrong").

Choose punchy action verbs, and make your sentence structure simple. Use examples where possible, and pull people in with stories.

Step 5: Check everything. Because of the Internet, everything you publish will be accessible for decades to come. You do not want an egregious error in your text. Have someone proof-read your article before turning it in to a publisher or editor. Better yet, send the article to other compliance professionals to get their comments and suggestions. Also, double-check any points of law or court decisions.

Step 6: Find a publisher. Finding a place to publish your article, book or blog post is easier than many people think. Consider magazines that cater to the compliance community, including Compliance Week and Compliance and Ethics Professional. Or, think about publishing on one or more of the highly respected blogs, like the Society of Corporate Compliance and Ethics Blog or the FCPA Blog.

You may also consider traditional newspapers like the Financial Times or a local paper. Try to find the name of the editor, and write to him or her directly. If you can, get permission to distribute a link to your article, so you can use it in the future for your self-marketing. You can also pitch your article to the legal press (for instance, Legal Week Magazine or

Thomson Reuters publishing). Another possibility is to publish your work on your own website or blog.

Step 7: Cross-promote and publicize your article. Take to social media and share your article wherever you can. Chapter 9 of this book is dedicated to using social media, and promoting your work on the web.

Step 8: Leverage your article. Post your article in more than one place, or use the research you did in creating your article as the basis for a speaking engagement or a panel discussion. Chapter 9 includes a section dedicated to re-purposing and leveraging your work on and offline.

Writing an article, blog post or book will give you instant credibility. If you are able to include a published article with your next job application, you will immediately give the impression of someone at the top of your field. There is very little that powerfully establishes creditability more than becoming a published author in the field.

Seven Steps to Creating a Successful Article

1. *Pick a topic you find interesting*

2. *Find a hook*

3. *Put yourself in the reader's shoes*

4. *Make the text sing*

5. *Check everything*

6. *Find a publisher*

7. *Cross-promote and publicize your article*

8. *Leverage your article*

Say It Like You Mean It

Studies have shown most people's greatest fear isn't fear of dying, it's fear of public speaking. Public speaking gives many people nightmares.

The thought of being in front of a critical audience leaves people feeling naked and exposed to ridicule. Just imagining being in front of a hundred listeners makes many people break into a cold sweat. However, the ability to speak effectively in public can change entire careers. Your willingness and desire to give conference presentations or keynotes will serve two exciting purposes: (1) It highlights your program, and shows that your company is serious about ethics and compliance, and (2) It shows you are an expert who can teach others about your field of expertise.

I spent my youth in theater, film and television. I had many experiences acting in front of audiences and cameras, so you might think presenting is easy for me. It's not. I become absolutely terrified before a big presentation. While I've become more confident with practice, I'm always a bit nauseated before a presentation, especially if it is one I haven't given before.

How does one become a conference presenter? This, like writing an article, is easier than you might think.

Steps to Becoming a Conference Speaker

Step 1: Identify a Conference. The first thing to do is to identify a conference at which you might speak. There are several ways to identify conferences. The first is to identify any conference that you have attended, then look up the organizer's website to find out about the submission process. If you haven't attended any compliance conferences, you could start with the Society of Corporate Compliance and Ethics (SCCE). The SCCE presents conferences all over the world. They have regional conferences, international conferences, and specialty conferences focusing on everything from oil and gas to internal audit's relationship with compliance.

If you are a member of the SCCE (and I highly recommend you join), you'll get emails periodically letting you know that conferences in your area are looking for speakers. You can also find information about speaking on the SCCE's website, www.corporatecompliance.org.

Compliance Week magazine hosts conferences in the United States and abroad, as does C-5 and PLI. Women in Compliance hosts conferences, as do various law firms and compliance-oriented vendors. You can also talk to compliance consultants (for example, KPMG, EY, Deloitte and PWC) to see if they are sponsoring any conferences in your area.

If you want to ease your way into speaking in front of people, you might consider volunteering to host a webinar for the SCCE or another organization before you choose to submit to present at a live conference.

Step 2: Decide on a Topic. Once you've decided on a conference at which you'd like to speak, review the topics presented at the most recent conference held by the group. Was the conference focused primarily on anti-bribery topics? Was there an emphasis on soft skills (communication, training, etc.), or was it entirely dominated by legal updates and discussion about the law? Your job is to select a topic that will appeal to the organizers. The best topics are usually similar to, but not a copy of, topics already chosen for previous conferences. Why is this? Because conferences tend to develop their own personalities, and the people who attend year after year will expect similar (but not carbon copy) experiences to the one they had the previous year.

When choosing a topic, you should pick one about which you are (1) knowledgeable, and (2) passionate. You will inevitably be putting some of your free time into creating your presentation, so you want to pick something that you will enjoy researching. Likewise, you want to be able to answer questions with relative ease, so you should pick a topic about which you have some knowledge.

What kind of topics can you choose? You can't go wrong with a legal update (e.g., the latest on anti-bribery law, data privacy regulation, trade sanctions, etc.). If you choose to do a legal update, you may want to co-present with a private practice lawyer who specializes in the topic you've chosen.

You can also provide a case study based on your company's activities. For instance, you could do a presentation on the lessons learned when your company implemented its whistle-blower hotline throughout Europe, or how it performed a privacy impact analysis in Asia when launching a new product. Be aware that many companies are uncomfortable with their compliance officer talking about the internal functioning of the company, so you will need to get explicit approval from your company before submitting a topic related to your company's internal actions.

You can present on a soft skills topic like communication, training, engagement, or presentation. You can also bring in another two or three experts to do a panel discussion on any topic you can imagine relating to compliance.

Step 3: Give Your Presentation a Catchy Title. If you give your presentation a catchy title, it will immediately intrigue people, and make your talk much more likely to be chosen (and to be a success when the talk is given). Catchy titles frequently include action verbs and evocative adjectives. Avoid corporate speak and compliance acronyms wherever possible. Wouldn't you rather go to a talk called, "Compliance Superstars — how to make your program shine with a limited budget" rather than "Incorporating Key Performance Indicators into your Board Strategy."

One of my favorite titles came from an annual SCCE conference: "Seven Years of Intimidation and Fraud ... Aftermath of a Rogue Leader." The title was instantly engaging. I wanted to know: (1) What was the fraud? (2) How was it discovered? (3) What did the compliance team do about it? (4) What lessons were learned? and (5) How does the compliance team operate differently after that experience? Use descriptive and interesting titles in order to excite the audience and make your talk more likely to be chosen.

Step 4: Draft the Bullet Points or Subtitles. Once you've created a title, you'll need to flesh out the talk with bullet points or subtitles. Most conferences require approximately three bullet points that describe your talk in more detail.

When drafting your bullet points, keep in mind how the people watching your talk will benefit from attending, and draft your bullet points from this point of view. Highlight how the audience members will be able to do their jobs more effectively, or how they will benefit from greater skills and knowledge because they watched your presentation.

Once again, action verbs and punchy adjectives are key, as is the use of plain language. One of my favorite examples came from a presentation given at the London conference of the SCCE several years ago. The talk promised to explore the challenges of an international environment, and the bullet point stated, "Learn how to respond effectively when dealing with difficult works councils, otherwise known as, 'Not France and Germany again!'" I loved it! As a practitioner in London who had been struggling to get the French and German offices of our company to agree to certain sections of our new draft Code of Conduct, I immediately wanted to attend this session.

Another tactic is to include rhetorical questions in your bullet points, with statements such as, "Do you struggle with giving advice to the business regarding which kinds of marketing emails can be sent under German data privacy law? This session will focus on simple, easily implemented strategies to ensure your business functions comply with the law." Questions engage the viewer, and offer him or her the opportunity to engage in a conversation with you in their minds, even though they aren't talking to you directly.

Putting together the bullet points or subtitles is important, as it gives you the opportunity to begin to outline your presentation. Most submission forms require your title, bullet points, a curriculum vitae or your resume, and a professional head and shoulders headshot. Be sure to keep your CV or resume up to date, and keep a good professional quality headshot on hand, so you can respond to calls for submissions quickly.

Step 5: Draft the Presentation. Congratulations! Your presentation has been accepted! It's now time to draft your presentation. Most presenters at conferences use PowerPoint slides to guide their presentations. You will likely want to create PowerPoint slides for your presentation as well.

When you first begin to create your presentation, I recommend writing down all of your ideas on paper. Don't edit yourself at this point. Instead, write down anything related to your topic that you think you could conceivably include in your presentation. Once you've exhausted your thoughts, start to place them into an order that makes sense. Take out or cross off any thought that doesn't belong, and strengthen the others. Try to separate your presentation into two or three main ideas.

Once you've got your ideas in order, it is time to draft your slides. Some very good presenters may not need slides, but usually you'll want a few to keep your presentation moving. Personally, I always use slides. I do this to give people something visual to look at that is changing throughout my talk. People can therefore be learning and engaged in both auditory and visual ways. I also try to use slides with humor or pictures, so that people are actively involved as the presentation goes by.

Please don't crowd your slides with text. The term "Death by Power-Point" comes to mind when I think of all the presentations I have attended where slides were crammed with too-small black-and-white text repeating exactly what the presenter is saying. When people see crowded text they either (1) stop listening and start reading, or (2) give up on the presentation. Use slides, but use them only for key words or pictures, so that your presentation has flow and you remember where you are in your narrative.

Also, please don't ever read your script. Use notecards if you must, but do not hold a script. When I'm doing a brand new talk on a topic I'm not sure about, I tend to write out an entire script, and then create the slides around the script. Then I create notecards, or practice enough that I don't need the script anymore. People will completely stop listening to you if you're simply reading a monologue. You are no longer authentic or exciting, as you now appear "scripted."

Step 6: Practice, Practice, Practice. I deliver my presentations out loud at least three times before I give them before an audience. My poor dogs and my husband have watched more talks on compliance programs and data protection law than any creatures in the universe should ever have to endure. If all else fails, practice in front of the mirror. I know many professionals think they can just wing it, or that they know their topic so well that they don't need to practice. That's nonsense. There is nothing like presenting your talk out loud to find out where there are difficulties. Rough transitions, slides that don't flow easily from one to another, and jokes that aren't funny can all be smoothed out when you practice out loud. You'll also learn where you need to do further research, or where you aren't as confident as you should be.

You deserve to do a great job at your presentation, and practice is the only way to do so. Try to get someone to let you give the speech to them while they write down feedback. Remember, your friend, spouse or neighbor will be kinder than the audience, so take the feedback as a gift to make you better.

Step 7: Prepare to Present. If you are able to, visit the room in which you will be presenting and stand at the podium or front of the room to see the view. Sometimes knowing where you'll be presenting can help you to visualize your speech going well.

Right before I present, my nerves go mad. I feel terrified, and I can't catch my breath. I've learned to deal with this by consciously breathing. I feel the breath go in and out, and I pay attention to my body. I always wear clothing in which I feel powerful. I often wear four- or five-inch heels when I'm presenting, as they make me stand up straight and make me taller, giving me more presence in the room.

I recommend you bring a plastic bottle of water with you onto the stage or in the front of the room. Don't assume that you will just use the water provided at the conference, as many presenters have been thrown off by trying to pour from unwieldy glass bottles into glasses that have a tendency to fall over.

I like to stand in the front of the room and welcome people as they arrive. I either verbally say hello, or give them big smiles while catching their eye. I want people to know I am happy they are here. If you stand in the front of the room before the presentation starts, staring at your phone, people will be much less engaged than they will be if you immediately take control of the room by standing in the front and smiling.

Step 8: Have a Great Opener. Studies have proven that speakers have somewhere between thirty seconds and one minute before the audience decides if they are interested in the rest of the presentation. Therefore, it is imperative that you open in a powerful way. Some suggestions include:

- If you're giving an update on a regulation, why not begin with a story describing the facts of the case? Use the present tense. If you're telling the story of a bribe, begin with, "It was a dark night in Sierra Leone when a shadowy man came through the door …" This opener is going to be far more engaging than, "OK ladies and gentlemen, today I'm going to give an update on the recent FCPA investigations …"

- Start with a question or series of questions. For example, if your topic is "Creating an Ethical Culture," start with "How many of you believe your companies' culture is the same throughout the world?" If you have access to the voting buttons and have the ability to display the results, people tend to be very engaged, as they see themselves directly involved and contributing to the conversation.

- Do something unexpected. I begin my presentation on selling compliance to an internal audience with the following, "Ladies and gentlemen, boys and girls, step right up to see the world's most fantastic invention. It's Compliance Glitter!!! Just sprinkle some compliance glitter on your board or your managers, and they'll be instantly compliant." This always immediately grabs people's attention. To keep the sense of surprise, I always plant someone in the audience. I continue, "See this man? His company was besieged with fines and malfeasance, but after using Compliance Glitter, his company is on the world's most ethical companies list. Don't believe me, just ask him!" At this point, the plant stands up and says, "Compliance Glitter worked for me!" This beginning creates real anticipation for what is to come. The remainder of the talk is full of serious information, but the beginning grabs people's attention so they keenly anticipate what may come next.

- If you can't create a catchy opening, at least thank the people who are listening for coming. Audiences enjoy being acknowledged, and their time and attention is a valuable gift. Tell the audience what you like about them or why you are happy to be there.

Step 8: Shine during the Presentation. If you're able to, you should move within a six- to nine-foot wide space across the stage. The only exception is in panel discussions, where you are likely going to be seated. If possible, stand during the presentation. Standing is more dynamic. Try to use the stage, as audiences will find you more engaging if you're moving a bit. Don't pace — use the space confidently.

Try to maintain eye contact with your audience. If you look people in the eye for one to three seconds each, they are likely to be engaged with you. This is another reason not to read from a script, as direct eye contact will dramatically increase your ability to relate to your listeners.

Don't be afraid to take small pauses. Seasoned presenters know a dramatic pause can be used to create anticipation and interest. New presenters sometimes feel that if they don't speak every moment, they're going to lose their place and not recover. Don't be afraid to take a beat or a breath when you change slides. Your audience is probably with you, and they want to reflect on what they've heard and prepare to receive the next part of the information. A pause can also be used as punctuation, or an opportunity to regain people's attention. A well-timed pause can make people look up from their phones to help them to re-engage. Use pauses to your advantage to add drama to your presentation.

Use everyday language and small words to connect with your audience. Powerful presentations using everyday language are easily understood. If you are using complex language, you risk losing your audience.

Step 9: Handle Questions and Answers with Ease. You should decide up front whether you want to take questions during the presentation, or after it has finished. If I am providing a highly scripted talk, I state up front that I will leave time for questions at the end. This allows people to relax and to listen to the whole presentation without trying to interrupt it. If I'm giving a regulatory update, or talking about difficult laws, I usually invite people to ask questions during the presentation, as I want to provide clarity throughout. Either way, invite your audience to ask questions so you can get their full engagement.

Question and answer sessions require you to pay attention to timing. Remember, as the person on stage, it is your job to control the audience and the tempo. I've seen many presenters get stuck answering every single question the audience has, and then not finish their presentation. This is poor time management, and will make you seem less effective than if you say, "Thank you for the questions; I'll take more as soon as we get through the next section." You are in control, and it is up to you to get through your material.

Step 10: Finish the Presentation on time. Be sure that in your practice you time the presentation so you can get through all of your slides or material. There is nothing more frustrating for an audience than to see you not finish the talk you prepared. Always wear a watch so you can see how much time you have, and always finish about one minute early. People get antsy when a talk runs over the allotted time, especially if they have somewhere to go and need to get up and leave. You will seem much more professional if you control the clock, finish your talk on time, and get through all of the promised topics and each of your slides. And, if you are taking questions at the end of your presentation, finish your presentation five minutes before the end time.

Step 11: Capitalize after the Talk. After the talk finishes, you should be prepared to stay to answer questions. I've been stopped with a line of people with questions or comments for up to an hour after a presentation, so ensure you don't have to leave immediately after your talk. Bring plenty of business cards, and if someone tries to monopolize you for too much time, offer to follow up with them by phone or email, so you can get through your line of questioners.

Public speaking can be terrifying, but it is an excellent way for you to build confidence in your expertise, and to demonstrate your knowledge to others.

Eleven Steps to Creating a Successful Presentation

1. *Identify a conference*

2. *Decide on a topic*

3. *Give your presentation a catchy title*

4. *Draft the bullet points or subtitles*

5. *Draft the presentation*

6. *Practice, practice, practice*

7. *Prepare to present*

8. *Shine during the presentation*

9. *Handle questions and answers with ease*

10. *Finish the presentation on time*

11. *Capitalize after the talk*

Those Who Can, Teach

There is an old adage that reads, "those who can, do, and those can't, teach." That's nonsense, especially when it comes to adjunct professorships. Many universities and law schools are actively looking for practitioners with real-world experience who will teach their students about the nuts and bolts of doing the job.

I'm a professor of Global Compliance and Ethics at Widener University, Delaware School of Law. I teach Masters of Jurisprudence students about international laws, along with practical lessons about their application to the compliance profession. It has been a joy to teach, and I have learned more by creating the syllabus, drafting and researching the lectures, and reading examinations, than I ever have performing my job.

How do you find a teaching position? One way is to simply call local colleges, community colleges, and universities, and offer to teach. You can write a cover letter and send your C.V. and hope for the best. You can also look for ways to be involved with a potential school, and to meet the deans. I have several friends who called their former law school or university to offer to teach. Law schools frequently have alumni teaching, as it showcases the talent and success of their alumni to their current students.

There are few things in life that make someone immediately respected as an authority on a subject faster than the title "Professor." If you can, teach.

Out for Glory – On Awards

"And the winner is...." It is truly wonderful to be recognized by your community for your excellence. There are a number of awards given out within the compliance environment, including the Thomson Reuters Regulatory Compliance Awards, the Women in Compliance Awards, the Rising Star in Corporate Governance Awards and the annual awards given by the Society of Corporate Compliance and Ethics. How do you win such an award? The first step is getting nominated.

Usually people want someone to decide out of the blue to nominate them, and then hope that the nominating individual knows enough about them to effectively write a letter that will showcase with specificity their career highlights and accomplishments. The trouble with this course of action is that even the most ardent best friend or co-worker rarely has a full picture of the skillset and accomplishments of the person they want to nominate.

How do you get around this problem? Easy – you either nominate yourself for an award, or you draft a highlight sheet with explanations of what you've done, and ask a friend to nominate you using the information you provide (along with anything else he or she wants to add). Why is this effective? You may very well be the best Junior Compliance Officer of the Year, but if your boss doesn't know that you also volunteered pro bono legal services to women in need in your community, you may not win the distinction simply because the information wasn't known.

Don't be ashamed to nominate yourself for awards. If you don't deserve to be shortlisted, then you won't be, and there will be no harm done. However, if you are shortlisted or if you win, you will once again confirm your status as an expert in your field.

My first year at UIP I was nominated for the Chief Compliance Officer of the Year Award at the Women in Compliance Awards. While I was at Gibson Dunn, the team I worked with was nominated for the Best Regulatory Law Firm of the Year Award. Although neither I nor Gibson Dunn won the award, the shortlisting provided great capacity to showcase our talents to the greater world.

This year I will be a judge at the Women in Compliance Awards. Being a judge has also brought with it notoriety and an implied endorsement of my skills and ability to evaluate greatness in the compliance profession. Remember the phrase, "no guts, no glory." Sometimes it takes guts to nominate yourself. The glory will be worth it in the end.

Putting It Together

One doesn't need to utilize all of these techniques to become recognized as an expert, but choosing one or two will help you break away from the pack of other compliance officers whenever you find yourself ready to move into your next job or promotion. With recognition comes respect from the business in which you work, and the ability to mentor junior peers in the industry.

Becoming an expert takes work and courage. It can take time and effort to perform the research required to write an article after you come home from work. It takes courage to decide to get up on stage in front of your peers to deliver a speech. However, the rewards can be enormous. Take courage, make a decision, and the designation "compliance expert" can be yours.

Chapter 9: Working the Industry Network

The phrase "It's not what you know. It's who you know" is good advice in any business, but for people working in compliance, there are many compelling reasons to grow and maintain your network.

Regulators throughout the world give credit and mitigate punishments when a company has a "good" or "effective" compliance program. But how does the regulator know what a "good" program looks like in your industry, country, or size of company? Regulators and prosecutors look at compliance programs every day to determine the benchmark for "good." Therefore, it is imperative you know the trends in the industry, and monitor and improve your program to the level expected by the regulators. If you assume your program is good enough, but you don't continually benchmark to determine the expectations of the regulators, you may be caught by surprise if you have a regulatory investigation.

The compliance profession is full of passionate and hard-working people, all of whom need to know how their programs stack up against each other. You can hire a consultant to give you this information, but that is expensive, and should only be done once every one to five years. In the meantime, your network can provide you with continual information to benchmark your own program.

How do you find people for your network? The first place to look is within your current business. You can network with the other compliance and legal people at your company, and in companies where you previously worked. You can and should reach out to people with whom you went to school, as well as people in networking and industry groups. Today, networking goes beyond the people you have met in person. The digital world creates tremendous opportunities to reach out to people all over the world.

This chapter will teach you how to make the most of the opportunities that present themselves at conferences, and will then explore how to make the most of the digital and social media world of compliance.

Working the Conference Room

Have you ever gone to a conference, only to hang around staring at your phone, praying that the day ends quickly? Have you tried to join a group of chatting people, only to find yourself not listening and hoping to go home as soon as possible? If so, you're not alone. However, you're missing a tremendous opportunity. Conferences can be a terrific place for networking, especially if you have a plan.

Keith Ferrazzi's masterful book, "Never Eat Alone," has an entire chapter dedicated to properly preparing for a conference.[23] When I began reading his book, I'd just been to my first Society of Corporate Compliance and Ethics conference in London. I didn't know anyone at the conference, and I felt awkward sitting by myself during lunch the first day. I'm embarrassed to admit it, but I didn't even stay for the networking reception at the end of the conference. I went home as soon as the last session ended. I wondered why I'd even bothered to spend all the time at the conference, when I could have been doing "real work" for my company. "What's the big deal about networking?" I wondered.

Six months after that conference in London, I attended the international conference of the SCCE in Washington D.C. The conference featured several of the speakers I'd seen in London, and I was excited to see those speakers again. I had something to talk about with the speakers that I recognized. By the time I left the Washington D.C. conference, I felt like I had new friends. Simply suffering through the first conference made the second conference much easier and more enjoyable.

So, the bad news is this — you may have to start your networking and conference attending without knowing anyone. But the good news is that once you've been to one event, the next one should be much easier.

Connecting with Connectors

There are always leaders in an organization or movement. These people often flit through the room, hugging others and introducing people to each other. These people are Connectors. If you watch carefully, you'll see who they are. You should make it your business to get to know them.

During the first SCCE conference I attended in London, I noticed a woman who talked to everyone. She glided through the room with people hanging on her every word. I was impressed. Not only had she given a terrific talk about transitioning from the mindset of a lawyer to that of a compliance officer, she clearly knew every important person in attendance. I decided that I needed to know her, and when I saw her in the lounge at the conference hotel in Washington D.C. six months later, I made it my mission to befriend her. She was then gracious enough to introduce me to several other leaders in the compliance world. By getting to know her, I was then able to meet others who have since helped my career in significant ways.

Every town and organization has Connectors. Make it your mission to identify them, and to befriend them or join their networks. Follow them on Twitter, befriend them on LinkedIn, or join a LinkedIn Group to which they belong (more on that later in the chapter). Send them a note asking them to go for coffee. Connectors enjoy meeting people, and will be happy to get to know you if you show them interest and respect their time.

Plan Your Attack and Hit List

You will get much more out of conferences if you plan beforehand. Conferences traditionally publish the names of all the speakers, and the organizations for which they work. Take time the week before the conference to determine who you would like to meet. You want to target people who: (1) work at a company or in an industry you find interesting, (2) have something in common with you (e.g., you went to the same college or you both live in the same city), or (3) are famous or important in your field. Choose three to five people you'd like to meet, then Google them. If you can find their LinkedIn profile, find out about their interests or previous roles. Plan a conversation starter, so that when you meet you have something catchy to say to engage the person in a conversation.

I used these techniques when I met Alexandra Wrage, the founder of TRACE International. I had admired Alexandra from the minute I joined the compliance and anti-bribery world. I was going to the Women in Compliance Awards in 2014 when I found out Alexandra would be at my table. I did not want to squander the opportunity to meet her, so I looked her up online. I found out that she lived in America but was Canadian, and had gone to school in Britain. I myself was born in Canada, lived in America for most of my life, and was living in London. As soon as I met Alexandra, we bonded over our shared experiences of living, studying and working in the three countries. Alexandra became a dear friend and mentor. By preparing for the evening, I made the conversation easy by having something specific to say. The following year, when I was nominated for the Chief Compliance Officer Award at the Women in Compliance Awards, Alexandra was the first person to send me a note of congratulations.

Once you've decided who you want to meet, you can reach out to the person before the conference. You can send the person an email saying you're looking forward to the event or to his or her session (if the person is a speaker), or you can tweet the individual saying you can't wait to see the individual's session. Lastly, you could write and make a plan to go to lunch, dinner, coffee or cocktails, if you really want to solidify the opportunity.

Keith Ferrazzi suggests planning a dinner or sightseeing event the night before the conference. He suggests inviting your closest friends, current associates, and the people you want to meet for a get-together. He loves this plan, as many people fly in for conferences and then have nothing to do the night before. Instead of sitting in a hotel room having room service, the VIPs could be having dinner with you and networking with your other contacts at the same time.

I haven't implemented Mr. Ferrazzi's plan yet, but I've seen a number of consulting firms and law firms organize such dinners. This strategy can be doubly effective, because not only does it put together a group of great people, it also makes you the hub of the group, demonstrating your value in connecting like-minded leaders.

Regardless of which techniques you choose, go to a conference with a plan. You'll gain much more from the networking opportunities if you've got a plan, instead of leaving it to chance.

Make the Most of Your Meetings

After the conference has concluded, be sure to follow up with everyone you met. Take the business cards you collected and send LinkedIn requests to connect, along with a personal note about how nice it was to meet the person at the conference. In order for networking to work for you in the long-term, you'll need to follow up immediately, and then at regular intervals after that. But how can you follow up with so many people? The answer is social media.

Social Media Synergies

I've met many compliance professionals who are afraid of social media. The reasons I've heard for avoiding it include:

- I have nothing interesting to say;
- I'm afraid I'll write something controversial or that my employer will be mad at me for something I write;
- I don't know how to use it;
- I don't think it works for people in the compliance profession;
- I don't want to increase my profile; and
- I don't want anything personal online.

While there is merit to some of these thoughts, the benefits you can accrue from participating in social media far outweigh the risks. A prudent compliance officer can greatly increase his or her knowledge by participating in social media. More outspoken compliance professionals can create content, comment, and become known in the field using social media.

Roy Snell, CEO of the Society of Corporate Compliance and Ethics, wrote an excellent post about the power of social media participation within the compliance community. He said, "The benefits of being active on social media are enormous. You can become a household name in the compliance social media world without ever posting anything that might be considered controversial. If you are trying to build a network and respect, in an effort to improve your position in our profession, social media can be invaluable."[24]

> *"If you are trying to build a network and respect, in an effort to improve your position in our profession, social media can be invaluable." – Roy Snell, CEO Society of Corporate Compliance and Ethics*

Social media connects you to the whole world. Once you join in, you'll be amazed to find a community of passionately committed compliance professionals from around the world sharing best practices. You'll also position yourself as a leader, which can make finding your next job much easier, because people feel they know you from your online presence.

Of course, one must be careful with social media and online branding. Compliance officers and lawyers have to watch what they say so that they do not offend their clients or the company for which they work. Likewise, it is generally recommended that compliance officers avoid posting pictures where they are visibly drunk or acting out. But with a bit of common sense, you can greatly increase your visibility within the compliance industry by participating in social media.

The following is a simple introduction to the ways that a compliance officer can use social media to connect to the global network. Whole books have been written regarding how to use each platform from a technical perspective, which is beyond the scope of this book. Likewise, there are many other social networks available beyond LinkedIn, Twitter and Facebook. However, for the purposes of a compliance officer, these are the three that will connect you rapidly to others in the compliance community.

LinkedIn

Every professional should have a profile on LinkedIn. LinkedIn can connect you to millions of other people at the touch of a button. It is likely that you've received requests to join LinkedIn via emails from friends or colleagues, and joining is simple. Make sure you add a professional photograph so that people can recognize you, especially if you have a common name. Once you add the details of your current and previous positions, voila! You are now on social media.

LinkedIn has made a tremendous difference in my life. I was found on LinkedIn by an in-house recruiter, which led to my job as Chief Compliance Officer at UIP. When I responded to the "In Mail" sent to me by the recruiter, I asked her why she had sought me out. She told me I was the only person in the London market that she could find that had a film and television degree, was a lawyer, and worked in compliance. Getting the top compliance job at UIP was directly related to the recruiter's ability to see that my undergraduate degree from UCLA was in film and television.

LinkedIn has also allowed me to virtually meet the most interesting people in my field. LinkedIn has a feature that will tell you if anyone in your network knows any other person on LinkedIn. Therefore, you can search for anyone you want to meet, and then you can find a way to get a warm introduction by asking one of your current contacts to introduce you. I've used this feature a number of times when I wanted to meet someone I hadn't come across yet in real life.

LinkedIn Groups

Once you have a LinkedIn profile, you've just scratched the surface of the LinkedIn world. LinkedIn has a feature where individuals can join groups. Some groups are closed, requiring you to request membership, but many are open to anyone. The Society of Corporate Compliance and Ethics, Compliance Week, and the Health Care Compliance Association all have active LinkedIn groups where compliance professionals participate. Most LinkedIn groups are used for posting information, especially articles, which other members read and find useful. One way to build a reputation quickly within the compliance community is to post articles or blog posts that you've written or enjoyed, so that the group members can benefit from them as well.

I belong to several LinkedIn groups. The groups I belong to relate to data privacy, the FCPA, anti-corruption, and compliance generally. I enjoy receiving emails from LinkedIn highlighting articles other group members have posted. About once a month I try to post an article I've found interesting, so that I'm contributing as well. I also enjoy commenting on other people's postings when the article is interesting.

Another benefit of joining LinkedIn groups is that you can post links to your speaking presentations, or to articles you've written. The occasional self-promoting post can do a lot for your visibility within the community. Additionally, other people in your LinkedIn group may be interested in your speech or session, and they may come to see you in person based on that information. It pays to post about your activities.

Twitter

Twitter is a microblogging service that connects you to the rest of the world through 140-character posts. When I first started on Twitter, I simply didn't understand how it worked. Of all the social media services, Twitter was the most unintuitive to me. But once I began to follow other compliance professionals and compliance-related companies, I found that the service was invaluable. Twitter users frequently create links to content other users would find useful. Now when I'm waiting for a meeting to start or sitting on the subway, I'm frequently looking at articles linked to me through Twitter.

Once you've set up your Twitter account, you should search for and follow journals, sites, and people in the field. Compliance Week Magazine (@complianceweek), the Society of Corporate Compliance and Ethics (@scce) and Wall Street Journal Risk and Compliance (@WSJRisk) are all good places to start. I'm @KristyGrantHart, and you are welcome to follow me as well!

As soon as you've begun to follow people relevant to the industry, you can retweet articles that you find interesting or helpful. You can also post links to content you enjoyed by using the Internet link and adding it to a tweet you create yourself.

Twitter is useful for creating relationships with people you may not have met in real life. I have begun Twitter conversations with several of the most prominent bloggers and thought leaders in the compliance industry by posting and commenting on their content via Twitter. In fact, just yesterday I was surprised when I looked on my LinkedIn profile and found that an FCPA thought leader and major publisher had looked up my profile after I tweeted some of his content on Twitter.

Facebook

Facebook can be a powerful place to grow your network, and to engage with people all over the world. Many people use their Facebook account for both business and personal uses. My Facebook page is private, and I keep it limited so that only my friends and family can see my posts.

However, many of my Facebook friends are also business contacts or people I have known at my previous jobs. When it comes to my career, Facebook helps me to celebrate my wins, including promotions, articles that are published, and speaking engagements.

Some people keep their Facebook account public so that anyone who wishes to see their page may access it. That is a matter of personal preference. In my experience, Facebook can be best used from a compliance career perspective by strengthening and deepening your relationships with people in the industry who are also your friends. Because of the more personal nature of Facebook, people become involved in your personal life in a way that can make them feel closer to you.

Personal Websites

Although it is relatively uncommon in the compliance field, some professionals are now creating personal websites to showcase their expertise. Thought leaders should always have a place where others can encounter their ideas. I created www.ComplianceKristy.com after I was nominated for the Chief Compliance Officer of the Year Award because I understood the benefit of a central place where I could collate the links on the web showing my speaking, writing, and media mentions. ComplianceKristy was created as a hub to provide connections for people who wanted to get to know me without having to surf through many different web links and websites.

You should consider creating a personal website if you want to stand out from the crowd, and make yourself a household name within the compliance world. This is especially true if you've started publishing articles and speaking. You may also consider starting a blog on your personal website. Many people have generated tremendous influence through a blog. Blogging is time-consuming, and, if you work for a traditional employer, you may have to be cautious about commenting on controversial topics. However, if you are comfortable creating interesting and thought-provoking commentary on a regular basis, you will quickly become known in the field.

The Power of Threes

Let's say you've come across an article with a really unique point of view on the latest trends in trade sanctions prosecution. You want to share it with your community, because you think others would find it enlightening and useful. How do you get the most leverage from the discovery? Try to post it on three different media. In the case of the trade sanctions article, I would post it to a relevant LinkedIn group to begin a discussion of the article. I'd also link to it via Twitter, and if it was appropriate as a resource for compliance officers, I would write a blog post about it and link to it from www.ComplianceKristy.com.

Different social media outlets have different audiences. You can shorten the time that it takes you to be regarded as a thought-leader or a curator of great content by posting interesting articles to more than one social media resource.

For example, I recently wrote an article for Compliance and Ethics Professional Magazine. The article was printed in the hard-copy version of the magazine that was sent to approximately 5,000 compliance professionals, but it wasn't available online. I contacted the SCCE and asked them to turn the article into a blog post which could be shared on social media. I then added the article's link as an update post to all of my LinkedIn contacts. Next, I posted the article to a LinkedIn group dedicated to the compliance industry. I also tweeted the link on Twitter, and posted it on my Facebook so that my family and friends could read it. In this way my one article was made available to several thousand people. Lastly, I embedded a copy of the article in my LinkedIn profile and added a link to my website (www.ComplianceKristy.com). As the article has been posted, I can now print color copies of it to send to clients and potential clients of Spark Compliance Consulting.

Because of social media, the time it took to write the one article for Compliance and Ethics Professional Magazine turned into the opportunity to reach thousands of people. I was able to use social media to vastly leverage the impact of the article by posting it multiple places.

We all have limited time. The best way to leverage the time you spend writing and speaking is to create multiple outlets and uses for the same product (article or speech) that you've created. Aim for the "power of three." If you can utilize your product three times, you've exponentially leveraged the time you've spent writing, researching or practicing, which means you can be even more Wildly Effective than before.

Chapter 10: Dealing with the Hard Stuff

Thus far we've dealt with the good stuff: how to influence people, how to make yourself an expert, and how to connect to the vast network of impassioned compliance professionals. But what about the bad days?

The compliance industry has an unusually high level of burnout. Many conferences showcase experts giving information about stress relief, work-life balance, and how to counteract the negative experiences that working in compliance can bring. This chapter deals with handling the bad times that will inevitably occur in your compliance career.

Feeling Defeated, Blamed, Misunderstood, Unappreciated, Hostile and Bored

There will unquestionably be days in the life of a compliance officer where the skies are grey and the tide is against you. Many compliance officers experience setbacks like the following:

Defeat: Compliance officers frequently need to fight for resources and support from the business. Sometimes an initiative will not be backed, or a policy decision will go the wrong way. It is easy to feel defeated when this occurs.

Blame: The job of a compliance officer was once described to me as, "You're the person who makes sure the trains run on time. No one notices when the train is on time, but when it is late, people throw a fit!" When executives, managers, or employees go through disciplinary actions for violating the rules, they often blame the compliance department, or you specifically, for their problems. You may experience shame or regret, even when you were doing the right thing.

Feeling Misunderstood: In many countries and industries, compliance is a brand new profession. People within your company and in your friend groups may not know what you do. Regrettably, some people aren't interested once they do know what you do! Being misunderstood can lead to feeling unimportant.

Under-appreciated: Many projects completed by a compliance officer are not outwardly appreciated. Registering and implementing a whistle-blower hotline throughout Europe is a major feat, yet it is unlikely to be met with cheers or a celebratory lunch, because businesses rarely think about celebrating compliance successes.

Hostility: When a new regulation or program is implemented, some business leaders may openly object to the controls the compliance officer puts in place. Stories abound of compliance officers trying to do the right thing, and being suppressed or even fired.

Boredom: When a compliance program is up and running, it can feel like every day is the same. Boredom can set in, and burnout may follow.

When these emotions take over from time to time, it is helpful to step back and remember your mission.

Connecting Back to Your Mission

When you feel really down, it is important to take the global view, and remember your mission. Your job as a compliance professional makes the world a better place. You are levelling the playing field for the small businessman or woman in an emerging market, because your due diligence procedures are making corruption less rampant, and rewarding companies with a reputation for fair dealing. You are making the world a better place by ensuring that your company abides by fair labor standards, and that supply chain audits occur to eliminate any possibility of your company engaging in modern-day slavery, or working with companies that employ forced labor.

Recently I was in Vietnam performing corporate training. During the weekend, I took a small boat tour down the river through the Mekong Delta into the rural South. There were only six travelers on our boat, including two Americans, two Germans, an Indonesian and a Frenchman. Our guide was named Kha, and he told us how his grandfather had been a high-ranking official in the Saigon embassy. Kha explained that he had a black mark against him because of his grandfather's actions aiding the Americans in the Vietnam War. He said the black mark lasts for three generations, and his son would not have one. Therefore, *he was saving up the $40,000 U.S. dollars it would take to buy his son a place on the police force so he could take bribes and be rich.* I was stunned. Kha's son's best choice is to be a bribe-taker. We must do better than that. I believe we can help make it so that Kha's son will have better choices.

When you feel defeated, remember each tiny action in the compliance space alters the corporate landscape in a way that is changing the world. The tiny little actions your company takes are made in concert with the actions of millions of other companies throughout the world. Companies, NGOs, and governments are changing the world, and you are on the front lines of this change. It is up to you to create the mechanisms, policies and procedures that protect your company from prosecution, but these same mechanisms, policies and procedures make the world a better place to live in for millions you may never meet.

When it all feels like it is going wrong, remember that you're making a difference by being on the side of law and ethics. Connecting to your underlying mission is critical, so you can keep going during the hard times.

Knowing When to Say, "That's not My Job!"

As you become a Wildly Effective Compliance Officer, people on the commercial side of the business will learn they can rely on you. This is generally a good thing, but you need to be clear where your mandate begins and ends. As a compliance officer, your job is to guide, counsel, profile risk, and put in procedures and policies to mitigate those risks. Your job is not to make commercial decisions.

When I was a young compliance officer, people in the business used to ask me to make decisions. I did not understand it was not my job to make the decisions. Rather, with a difficult commercial decision, my job was to profile the risks involved, and perhaps to make a recommendation based on my analysis of that risk. My job was NOT to tell them what to do, or to make the decision for them. Thank goodness my boss, the Senior Vice President of Global Compliance, taught me when to say, "That's not my job." She would gently say to the business, "These are the risks I've identified. The final choice is yours, based on your risk appetite, and how much this deal means to you."

To be clear, you MUST give clear and specific advice if the topic involves illegal or unethical activity. However, many questions you will face involve company policy or new ideas, and these must be evaluated according to risk. There isn't always a right or wrong answer, and in many cases it is not your job to make the final decision. That having been said, how do you decide when it is up to you to decide what to do?

Use the Compliance Officer Decision Tree

I developed the Compliance Officer Decision Tree after dealing with a high-ranking corporate executive who did not understand what I did and was not interested in learning what I did. After a particularly ugly conversation wherein she expected a commercial decision from me, I developed the Compliance Officer Decision Tree and shared it with her to help her to understand when she, as the business leader, needed to make the decision. I wanted her to understand when I had veto power, when it was my job to evaluate risks, and when it was my job to implement policies and procedures to mitigate risk. I used this Decision Tree to guide communications with her.

For every question or scenario the business brings you, use the Compliance Officer Decision Tree to help you determine whether or not you should be making the final decision. This should help you to clarify your role. When you are new in your job, or dealing with a boss that does not understand your job, use this Decision Tree to help you to draw your boundaries appropriately.

Compliance Officer Decision Tree

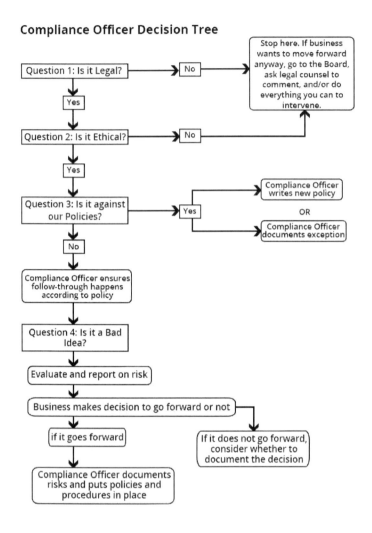

By going through the Decision Tree, you will be able to give the proper answer, and leave the commercial decisions to the business (where they belong). You may have to teach the business about your job. You may need to educate the men and women who you work with what your job entails. But this will be time well spent. Both you and the business will be happier when you understand the roles you both play in making the company successful.

Accepting Defeat

Sometimes, even when you put forth your best argument, the business will decide to go in a direction you know is either unethical or illegal. If the business is engaging in an illegal activity, it is in your best interest to continue taking the issue up through management until you get to the CEO or Board. If the CEO or Board accepts the risks relating to the illegal activity, you may need to get a new job. In recent times the United States Securities and Exchange Commission and the United Kingdom Serious Fraud Officer have held compliance officers personally liable when they did not properly implement and maintain their compliance program. For your own protection, you may need to accept that you can't win every battle, and leave when your reputation could be on the line. You may also need to consult a personal lawyer to ensure you don't have a reporting obligation and to protect yourself.

If your defeat is not a legal or ethical issue, but a question of policy, or whether something is a good idea, you must then decide whether to move forward in the best way possible while mitigating risk, or to start looking for a new job. The life of a compliance officer has many defeats. You may want to stick around to see what happens. Many times I've watched the business choose to go its own way against my counsel, only to see the business change its mind half-way through the activity.

Accepting Criticism

When you're doing your very best, it may be hard to hear that you could do your job in a more effective way. I used to hate receiving criticism, but Jack Canfield, author of "The Success Principles," completely changed the way I view it. Instead of viewing criticism as punishment, view it as information you can use to be more effective.[25]

> *Instead of viewing criticism as punishment, view it as information you can use to be more effective.*

Often people deliver criticism in an unhelpful way, but many times the underlying message is useful for your growth and development.

For instance, if during your annual review, your boss says that you don't speak up enough during meetings, you might hear that as criticism. You might even argue with her in your head about how she never asks you what you think, or that Bob in accounting always takes up half the meeting, so there is no time for you to say anything. Perhaps those things are true, but by taking the criticism as information and not getting defensive, you can evaluate how you could be more effective. You could, for instance, decide that in the future you will speak up at least twice during each meeting, and give yourself a check-mark on your notes each time you do to ensure you follow through.

Criticism can sting, but it can also make you better at your job. Jack Canfield implores people to seek out criticism, and to ask for it honestly. If you do this, be prepared to listen carefully, and not to respond defensively. If you do this successfully, people will trust that you want to improve, and will be honest with you, which can only make you better. Thank people who criticize you. They are helping you to become more effective.

Vacation: All I Ever Wanted

Sometimes the best way to become re-energized about your job is to take a break from it.

Regardless of how important your work is, you need to take vacation days. Even if you simply stay home and go for a long walk or watch a bunch of movies, you need to take time away from your job. The work of a compliance officer can be grueling, monotonous and conflict-ridden.

Time away from work reminds you that there is a great big world out there, and the mini-moments of strife at your job are not that important in the grand scheme of things.

Many entrepreneurs and spiritual thinkers report that their best ideas come when they have stopped focusing on work. Have you also noticed solutions to your problems tend to come when you're out walking your dog, playing with your kids in the park, watching TV, or waking up from sleep? Many people have breakthrough ideas while in the shower. Sometimes you must get out of your work environment to create room for your subconscious to work on a solution to the problem. Vacation is an extended time for sorting through your issues. Being in a new or novel environment allows your mind to think differently, making you more effective, not less.

It is especially important to take vacation if you are starting to feel burnt out. Vacation can revitalize your batteries, and your employer would much rather you spend two weeks away from the office recharging than having you quit because you don't want to keep going to work.

To make sure you take vacation time, follow these tips:

Plan Early and Put It on the Calendar: Ask for your vacation days at the beginning of the year. Once the boss has agreed to them, it is much less likely that you will run into objections. Also, putting the dates on your calendar and blocking them out means you've committed to them, and are more likely to follow through.

Remind Your Co-Workers a Month in Advance: Remind your boss and co-workers that you will be taking time off. Do not schedule meetings or phone calls for the time you'll be on vacation, if at all possible.

Choose a Time to Plug In: Ideally, you would be able to shut down the computer and iPhone/Blackberry/mobile device. However, in many compliance officer jobs, this is just not possible. So, pick a specific time of day when you will answer emails, and stick to it. I tend to answer emails after breakfast when on vacation, then I leave my mobile device in my hotel room and pick it up again once before bed. If you carry your device with you at all times, you will train your boss and co-workers that you are always available on vacation, defeating the purpose of being gone. Do not train people that you are available while on vacation.

Choose an Inaccessible Location: When I was in my 20s, a Vice President at the company I worked for planned her honeymoon in a remote corner of Laos. When I asked her why she chose Laos, she said it was because there was no cell phone or Internet reception there. Similarly, several lawyer friends of mine go camping each year in places without electricity. Others go on cruises in the ocean where WiFi service is not available. If you really can't bring yourself to unplug, pick a holiday location where you can't plug in.

Use the Out of Office Functions: Ensure that others' expectations are managed by putting on an automatic response or out-of-office email that tells everyone you are on vacation and will not be responding immediately. People are much more likely to respect your holidays if you let them know that you aren't available. Be sure to include a secondary resource, so that they can find help without following up with you. For example, "I am out of the office on vacation from October 1-10, and I will have limited access to email. If you need immediate assistance, please contact Sarah Banes at myassistant@com.com. I will get back to you as soon as I am able."

Respect Other People's Vacation Time: When your junior compliance officers or others are on their vacations, you should respect their time, and avoid sending them emails whenever possible. If you must send emails, send them with a note saying that the issue can wait until they return from holiday. Be the example.

If all else fails, try to remember that all the business decisions are ultimately not yours to make, and the world will not end if you need to leave your current job. You are not your job, and the stresses of your job should stay at your office and not come home with you every night.

A Silver Lining to Catastrophe

If, despite your best efforts, your company gets into dire trouble, is there any upside for you? Will you be forever tarred as an incompetent compliance officer who did not protect the company? Hardly. Unless you were genuinely not performing your job, there are silver linings to even the most public corporate failure.

You Are More in Demand After the Hurricane

Before I started Spark Compliance Consulting, I was considering changing jobs. I met with a recruiter to find out about the market. She asked if I'd been through any public meltdowns at any company where I had worked. I was surprised to hear her say, "Were there any major fines? Publically-acknowledged bribery investigations? Prosecution for fraud, bribery, competition violations? The more public the better. Companies are looking for compliance leaders who have been through the hurricane."

Why would a company actively look for someone who has been through major problems? Well first, companies want to know that if they have a public crisis, you have experience handling such a situation. They want to know they can rely on you to manage the public and internal chaos that comes with a bribery allegation or major disclosure. Second, companies want to know that you have real-world knowledge of required procedures and policies. If you've experienced what happens when things go wrong, you will be in a much better position to tell a company what is required so things won't go wrong.

Blessings of the Monitor

A Monitor is a court-appointed person, usually a lawyer, in charge of ensuring a company complies with the promises it made to the court or prosecutor. A "monitorship" is the length of time the company is under the watch of the Monitor. Monitorships are generally imposed when a company has done the wrong thing (usually committed bribery, but sometimes monitors are assigned in trade sanction actions or anti-trust/competition actions as well). The Monitor is an independent person who has the power to investigate whether the company is keeping the promises it made. Monitors typically have a slew of lawyers working with them to do the leg work. Monitors then report back to the government or court. If the company fails to keep the promises it made in resolving the action, the monitorship may be extended, or a company that was granted leniency may have the leniency revoked, and face prosecution.

Monitors get a bad name. Because the Monitor has so much power to perform investigations and to bill hours at a highly expensive rate, companies have pushed back and complained bitterly about the control the Monitor can exert. Monitorships can be quite expensive, and the company has little choice but to pay the bills and do as the Monitor requests.

I've worked twice as counsel for a Monitor. And while a monitorship can be burdensome, it can also create a golden opportunity for an in-house compliance officer. Remember the mantra, "Never let a good crisis go to waste." A company for which my friend works had a four-year monitorship imposed on it after being prosecuted for foreign bribery. In the wake of the imposition of the Monitor, my friend was able to access resources and buy-in from the business like never before. She was able to increase her access to the Board of Directors, and ensure she and her team were invited to leadership meetings.

If you work for a company that has been in trouble, or one that has been assigned a Monitor, rejoice! There is nothing like the pressure of a Monitor to make compliance front-and-center in the business. Even when things appear to have gone wrong, for the savvy compliance officer, everything may have gone right.

Chapter 11: Putting It All Together to be Wildly Effective

Congratulations on reaching the end of the book! I truly hope it has inspired you to think and act as a Wildly Effective compliance officer.

You've learned how to share your belief in your mission, and committed yourself to becoming more effective by using the Four Primary Motivators with your Power Sources. You've evaluated your training strategies, and added stories that will emotionally affect everyone who hears you. You're determined to dedicate time to becoming known as an expert in your field, and you've worked your network to benchmark your program more effectively. I hope that in the process, you've connected deeply to your desire to change the world. You are part of an army of corporate compliance people all over the planet who are making the world a better place, one training session at a time.

Top Ten Strategies

There is a great deal of information in this book, but if you keep the following top ten strategies in mind, you will inevitably be Wildly Effective.

Number 1: Believe in the mission of your compliance program with all your heart. If you don't believe in the program that you want to create (or have created), you cannot be Wildly Effective. Belief in your program will inspire that belief in others, creating buy-in and excitement for what you are doing.

Number 2: Use the Four Primary Motivators to leverage the Power Sources. Once you've determined the Power Sources' Primary Motivators, use this knowledge to get emotional buy-in from the Power Sources. Include examples from each Primary Motivator in all of your group and online training.

Number 3: Use the Wildly Effective Compliance Officer Risk Matrix to determine the proper approach for your company. Depending on the level of need for change, and the readiness of your company for change, you can make yourself much more effective by knowing how to frame your approach.

Number 4: Build critical bridges to the business through active listening, befriending individuals and humanizing yourself. You will be far more effective if people in the business like you and relate to you as an individual, instead of fearing you or staying away from you because you seem like the organization's police.

Number 5: Continually showcase your accomplishments and progress. Create a Compliance Dashboard to showcase your monthly accomplishments and your progress toward your annual goals.

Number 6: Become a good public speaker and known expert in the compliance field. Write articles or blog posts, give sessions at compliance conferences, put yourself up for awards, and comment on industry-related happenings.

Number 7: Develop your network of other compliance professionals, so you can benchmark your program and get support. Being a compliance officer can be a lonely and difficult job. Create and develop your network of other compliance professionals in order to properly benchmark your program, and receive support when you need it.

Number 8: Use social media to develop your expertise and sharpen your knowledge. Social media can connect you with thousands of other compliance professionals. Following the right LinkedIn groups will allow you to be up-to-date on trends in the profession, and on new regulations as they come out.

Number 9: Use the Compliance Officer Decision Tree to determine when to say "that's not my job." Sometimes the business will want you to make choices for them that are not appropriate for your remit. Use the Compliance Officer Decision Tree to determine when to push back to force the business to make the decisions.

Number 10: Remember that you are part of the mission to change the world. Ultimately, the compliance profession is made up of men and women who are making the world a fairer place. Be proud of the profession, and what it means to millions of people around the world who are counting on you to contribute to making the world a better place.

Jogging Down the Extra Mile to a Better World

Zig Ziglar said, "There are no traffic jams on the extra mile." By working hard to become a Wildly Effective compliance officer, you are jogging down the extra mile to a better world. You've chosen to study in-depth techniques that will make you an asset to your company and to the profession.

Thank you so much for joining me on this journey. As we jog together down the extra mile toward a better world, I hope you find your job easier and your influence greater because of the tips, tricks and techniques you've learned in this book. Congratulations!

Top Ten Tips

Believe in the mission of your compliance program with all your heart.

Use the Four Primary Motivators to leverage the Power Sources.

Use the Wildly Effective Compliance Officer Risk Matrix to determine the proper approach for your company.

Build critical bridges to the business through active listening, befriending individuals and humanizing yourself.

Continually showcase your accomplishments and progress.

Become a good public speaker and known expert in the compliance field.

Develop your network of other compliance professionals so you can benchmark your program and get support.

Use social media to develop your expertise and sharpen your knowledge.

Use the Compliance Officer Decision Tree to determine when to say "that's not my job."

Remember that you are part of the mission to change the world.

Acknowledgements

Writing a book was more of a journey than I ever could have imagined. Without the love and support of my family, mentors, and friends, it would not have been possible.

First I must thank my beloved husband Jonathan Grant-Hart. Your warmth, enthusiasm, and belief in me makes everything in my life possible. Thank you.

Thank you also to my family. My mother Kathy Elwood, father Kerry S. Grant, step-mother Linda Grant, and step-father Michael Elwood have offered immense love and support. Mom, your continual cheerleading and belief in me has made me able to soar. Thank you. Kelly Wood and Kimberly Black, I wouldn't be the woman I am today without you. You are wonderful sisters and I love you so much.

I'd also like to thank my mentors in the legal and compliance field, especially Lisa Beth Lentini, who gave me my first compliance role. You showed me how to do it, and I am deeply grateful for your guidance and friendship. I'd also like to thank Debra Wong Yang, Steve Sletten, Patrick Doris, and everyone at Gibson, Dunn & Crutcher for teaching me how to be a great lawyer.

Thank you to the Godfather of Compliance, Joe Murphy, who provided me with tremendous advice, editing and support throughout the revision process.

I'd like to thank my editor and friend Erin Larison for her tireless effort in finalizing this book.

Thank you to Karen Luniw, the world's most powerful coach. You've helped me to believe this was possible.

And lastly, I'd like to thank my friends who have joined me on my life journey and made each step possible, especially Natalie Leon Walsh, Marnie Smilen, Jenny Zdenak, Michele Moore Fried, Rachel Mendoza, Alison Charbonneau, Christopher Van Etten, Lisa Hall and Megan Tepper. You are the best friends a girl could ask for.

Kristy Grant-Hart is an expert in creating and implementing effective international compliance programs for multi-national companies. She is a speaker, author, professor, and thought leader in the compliance profession. She is the founder and Managing Director of Spark Compliance Consulting, a company focusing on creating, implementing and optimizing compliance programs, with a special focus on helping American companies to comply with European data privacy laws and the Modern Slavery Act.

Ms. Grant-Hart formerly served as Chief Compliance Officer for United International Pictures, the joint distribution company for Paramount Pictures and Universal Pictures, based in London. While there she was shortlisted for the 2015 Chief Compliance Officer of the Year award at the Women in Compliance Awards.

Ms. Grant-Hart is an Adjunct Professor at Widener University, Delaware School of Law, teaching Global Compliance and Ethics to Masters of Jurisprudence students. Ms. Grant-Hart began her legal career at the international law firm of Gibson, Dunn & Crutcher, where she worked in the firm's Los Angeles and London offices.

Ms. Grant-Hart graduated summa cum laude from Loyola Law School in California. She holds certification as a Corporate Compliance and Ethics Professional – International (CCEP-I) and is a member of the California Bar. She lives in London with her husband and beloved rescue dogs, Samuel and Mr. Fox.

Index

Notes

[1] U.S. News & World Report, Best Business Job, Compliance Officer, http://money.usnews.com/careers/best-jobs/compliance-officer.

[2] Sam Fleming, The age of the compliance officer arrives, The Financial Times (April 24, 2014), http://www.ft.com/cms/s/0/cadd54a6-c3bd-11e3-a8e0-00144feabdc0.html#axzz3b4IvXqdt.

[3] Press Release, Society of Corporate Compliance and Ethics, SCCE and HCCA combined membership reaches 15,000 (March 24, 2015) http://www.corporatecompliance.org/Resources/View/ArticleId/5373/SCCE-and-HCCA-combined-membership-reaches-15-000-1-2.aspx.

[4] Jill Treanor, JP Morgan Chase hires 3,000 new staff in its compliance department, The Guardian (Sept. 17, 2013), http://www.theguardian.com/business/2013/sep/17/jpmorgan-banking.

[5] Juliet Samuel, HSBC hires 3,000 as banks rush to bolster compliance, The Times (Sept. 25, 2013), http://www.thetimes.co.uk/tto/business/industries/banking/article3878201.ece.

[6] Lanny A. Breuer, United States Assistant Attorney General, Remarks at the New York City Bar Association (Sept. 13, 2012) (transcript available at http://www.justice.gov/opa/speech/assistant-attorney-general-lanny-breuer-speaks-new-york-city-bar-association).

[7] Noah J. Goldstein, Steve J. Martin, Robert B. Cialdini, Yes! 50 Scientifically Proven Ways to Be Persuasive (Free Press 2008).

[8] Lois P. Frankel, Nice Girls Don't Get The Corner Office (Hatchett Book Group 2004).

[9] Matt Levein, BNP Compliance Officers Were Fine With Some Non-Compliance, Bloomberg View (July 1, 2014), http://www.bloombergview.com/articles/2014-07-01/bnp-compliance-officers-were-fine-with-some-non-compliance.

[10] Leil Lowndes, How to Make Anyone Fall in Love with You (McGraw Hill 1996).

[11] Noah J. Goldstein, Steve J. Martin, Robert Cialdini, Yes! 50 Scientifically Proven Ways to be Persuasive 48-49 (Free Press 2008).

[12] Id.

[13] Id., pg. 42-44

[14] Id., pg. 43

[15] David Mattson, The Sandler Rules 5 (Pegasus Media World 2009).

[16] Goldstein, Yes! At 83 quoting Ben Franklin, The Autobiography of Ben Franklin (J. Bigelow, ed.) Philadelphia: Lippincott (originally published in 1868).

[17] Goldstein, Yes! at 85.

[18] Id. at 87

[19] Id.

[20] Id. at 151

[21] Id.

[22] Sheryl Sandberg, Lean In: Women, Work and the Will to Lead 28-29 (Alfred A. Knopf 2013).

[23] Keith Ferrazzi, Never Eat Alone and Other Secrets to Success, One Relationship at a Time (Doubleday Inc. 2005).

[24] Roy Snell, Using Social Media to Improve Your Position in Our Profession, The Compliance and Ethics Blog, available at http://compliance-andethics.org/using-social-media-to-improve-your-position-in-our-profession/

[25] Jack Canfield, The Success Principles (Harper Collins 2005).